D0855115

Project Management

Project
Management
A Financial
Perspective

Dr. Jae K. Shim, MBA, Ph.D.

Professor of Accounting and Information Systems
California State University, Long Beach
and
CEO, Delta Consulting Company

GLOBAL
professional
publishing

Global Professional Publishing Ltd
Random Acres
Slip Mill Lane
Hawkhurst
Cranbrook
Kent TN18 5AD
Email: publishing@gppbooks.com

ISBN 978-1-906403-57-7

Printed by Good News Digital Books

Table of Contents

Preface

Project Management: A Financial Perspective is designed to provide you with a deep understanding of the applications and importance of Project Management. You will learn how to assess a project with respect to time, costs, and resources in order to effectively and efficiently reach your goals. You will become familiar with the five processes involved in Project management – Initiating, Planning, Executing, Controlling, and Closing on time and within budget-- along with the nine knowledge areas – Project Integration, Project Scope, Project Time, Project Cost, Project Quality, Project Human Resources, Project Communications, Project Risk Management, and Project Procurement – that are essential to being an expert Project Manager.

Individuals need hard knowledge and real skills to work successfully in a project environment and to accomplish project objectives. This book is intended to equip its users with both. How? By explaining concepts and techniques and by illustrating through numerous examples how they can be skillfully applied.

This book is intended for students as well as for working professionals and volunteers. It is designed to outfit these people with the essential skills needed to make effective contributions and will have an immediate impact on the accomplishment of projects in which they are involved.

This book for the most part follows the framework within the Project Management Institute's Project Management Body of Knowledge (PMBOK). The material, however, places a financial focus on projects as a way to accomplish desired changes in the enterprise in a coordinated and predictable way for favorable outcomes. Topics covered include economic feasibility study, life-cycle costing, target costing, and earned value analysis. Through better project management, you can reduce or eliminate failed projects and reduce the costs associated with successful ones, resulting in increased enterprise effectiveness in providing the maximum value to shareholders.

ABOUT THE AUTHOR

Dr Jae K Shim

Dr. Jae K. Shim is one of the most prolific accounting and finance experts in the world. He is a professor of accounting and finance at California State University, Long Beach and CEO of Delta Consulting Company, a financial consulting and training firm. Dr. Shim received his M.B.A. and Ph.D. degrees from the University of California at Berkeley (Haas School of Business). Dr. Shim has been a consultant to commercial and nonprofit organizations for over 30 years.

Dr. Shim has over 50 college and professional books to his credit, including, *Barron's Accounting Handbook, Barron's Dictionary of Accounting Terms, 2011 GAAP: Handbook of Policies and Procedures, Budgeting Basics and Beyond, 2010-2011 Corporate Controller's Handbook of Financial Management, US Master Finance Guide, Uses and Analysis of Financial Statements, Investment Sourcebook, Dictionary of Real Estate, Dictionary of International Investment Terms, Dictionary of Business Terms, The Vest-Pocket CPA, The Vest-Pocket CFO,* and the best-selling *Vest-Pocket MBA*.

Thirty of his publications have been translated into foreign languages such as Chinese, Spanish, Russian, Polish, Croatian, Italian, Japanese, and Korean. Professor Shim's books have been published by CCH, Barron's, John Wiley, McGraw-Hill, Prentice-Hall, Penguins Portfolio, Thomson Reuters, Global Publishing, American Management Association (Amacom), and the American Institute of CPAs (AICPA).

Dr. Shim has also published numerous articles in professional and academic journals. He was the recipient of the Financial Management Association International's 1982 Credit Research Foundation Award for his article on cash flow forecasting and financial modeling.

Dr. Shim has been frequently quoted by such media as the *Los Angeles Times, Orange County Register, Business Start-ups, Personal Finance,* and *Money Radio*. He also provides business content He also provides business content for CPE e-learning providers and for m-learning providers such as iPhone, iPad, iPod, Blackberry, Android, Droid, and Nokia.

Email: drjaekshim@gmail.com, jaeshim@csulb.edu;
Web: www.csulb.edu/~jaeshim

CHAPTER 1

Overview of Project Management

A project is a temporary endeavor undertaken to achieve a particular aim (such as to create a unique product or service), and to which project management can be applied, regardless of the project's size, budget, or timeline. It is the response to a need, the solution to a problem. A project is defined as a problem scheduled for solution.

As defined in *A Guide to the Project Management Body of Knowledge* (PMBOK® Guide), project management is the application of knowledge, skills, tools, and techniques to a broad range of activities in order to meet the requirements of a particular project. Project management is comprised of five processes – Initiating, Planning, Executing, Controlling, and Closing – as well as nine knowledge areas. These nine areas center on management expertise in Project Integration, Project Scope, Project Cost, Project Quality, Project Human Resources, Project Communications, Project Risk Management and Project Procurement.

The phrase "project management" emerged in the late 1950s and early 1960s when the size, scope, duration, and resources required for new projects began to deserve more analysis and attention. Today, project management is used globally by multibillion-dollar corporations, governments, and smaller organizations alike. It serves as a means of meeting customers' or constituents' needs by both standardizing and reducing the basic tasks necessary to complete a project in the most effective and efficient manner. As a result, project management leadership is an increasingly desirable and sought-after skill as intense global competition demands that new projects and business development be completed on time and within budget.

The Steps in Managing a Project

The actual steps to manage a project are straightforward. Accomplishing them may not be. The model in Exhibit 1 illustrates the steps. Subsequent chapters of this book will elaborate on how each step is accomplished. The following is a brief description of the actions involved.

Define the Problem

As was discussed previously, you need to identify what the problem is that is to be solved by the project. It may help to visualize the desired end result. What will be different? What will you see, hear, taste, touch, or smell? (Use sensory evidence if things can't be quantified.) What client *need* should be satisfied by the project?

Develop Solution Options

How many different ways might you go about solving the problem? Brainstorm solution alternatives (you can do this alone or as a group). Of the available choices, which do you think will best solve the problem? Is it more or less costly than other suitable options? Will it result in a complete or partial fix?

Plan the Project

Planning is answering questions—what must be done, by whom, for how much, how, when, and so on. Obviously, answering these questions often requires a crystal ball. Answering these questions requires organizational skills applied to realistic thinking, and may in some cases require special knowledge of the project or a special skill set.

Execute the Plan

Once the plan is drafted, it must be implemented. Interestingly, we sometimes find that people go to great effort to put together a plan, and then fail to follow it. If a plan is not followed, there is not much point in planning. No plan, no control.

Monitor and Control Progress

Plans are developed so that end results may be achieved successfully. Unless you monitor your progress, you cannot be sure you will succeed. It would be like having a road map to a destination but not following the route to your destination. Needless to say, if a deviation from the plan is discovered, you must ask what must be done to get back on track and what caused the deviation to occur so as to be better prepared to avoid another setback in the future. If it seems impossible or unreasonable to return to the original plan, you must determine what modifications must be made to adapt to the new realities.

Close the Project

Once the destination has been reached, the project is finished, but you should take one final step. Some people may call it an audit, a review, a postmortem, and so on. The point is to look back on the project as a source of learning and improving the process the next time around. An easy way to do this is to ask yourself some simple questions. Note the way the questions are phrased. What was done well? What could have been improved? What were some of the best parts of the project plan? What did I contribute to the success of the plan? How could I improve? What else did we learn? The important thing in this stage is realizing that there is always room for improvement in ourselves. However, asking "What did we do wrong?" is likely to elicit a defensive reaction so the focus should always be on improvement, not on placing blame.

Exhibit 1: The Steps in Project Management

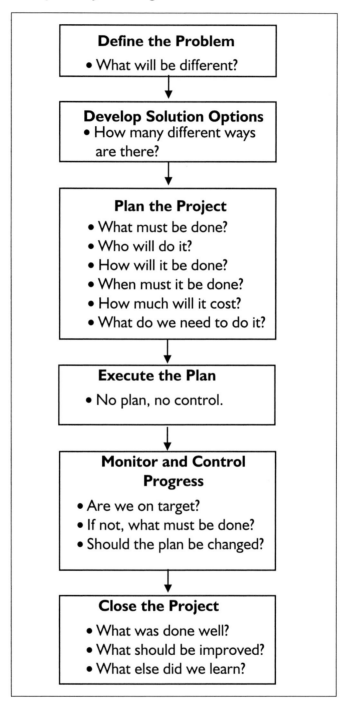

Define the Problem
- What will be different?

Develop Solution Options
- How many different ways are there?

Plan the Project
- What must be done?
- Who will do it?
- How will it be done?
- When must it be done?
- How much will it cost?
- What do we need to do it?

Execute the Plan
- No plan, no control.

Monitor and Control Progress
- Are we on target?
- If not, what must be done?
- Should the plan be changed?

Close the Project
- What was done well?
- What should be improved?
- What else did we learn?

The Project Management Body of Knowledge (PMBOK®)

The Project Management Institute (www.pmi.org) has attempted to define a minimum body of knowledge that a project manager needs in order to be effective. At present, PMI identifies nine general areas of knowledge, which are summarized below.

The nine areas of knowledge are the following:

1. *Project integration management.* Project integration management ensures that the project is properly planned, executed, and controlled. It includes the exercise of formal project change control.

2. *Project scope management.* Project scope defines the magnitude or size of the job. Changes to project scope are often the factors that kill a project. Scope management includes authorizing the job, developing a scope statement that defines the boundaries of the project, subdividing the work into manageable components with deliverables, verifying that scope planned has been achieved, and implementing scope change control procedures.

3. *Project time management.* Time management implies personal and combined efforts to manage progress over time. For projects, this amounts to developing a schedule that can be met, then controlling work to ensure that it is.

4. *Project cost management.* This involves estimating the cost of resources, including people, equipment, materials, and items such as travel and other support details. After this is done, costs are budgeted and tracked to keep the project within that budget.

5. *Project quality management.* One cause of project failure is the tendency to overlook or sacrifice quality in order to meet a tight deadline. It is not very helpful to complete a project on time, only to discover that the thing delivered won't work properly. Quality management includes both quality assurance (planning to meet quality requirements) and quality control (steps taken to monitor results to see whether they conform to requirements).

6. *Project human resource management.* Managing human resources is often overlooked in projects. It involves identifying the people needed to do the job; defining their roles, responsibilities, and reporting relationships; acquiring those people; and then managing them as the project is executed.

7. *Project communications management.* As the title implies, communication management involves planning, executing, and controlling the acquisition and dissemination of all information relevant to the needs of all project

stakeholders. This information includes project status, accomplishments, events that may affect other stakeholders or projects, and so on.

8. *Project risk management.* Risk management is the systematic process of identifying, analyzing, and responding to project risk. It includes maximizing the probability and consequences of positive events and minimizing the probability and consequences of adverse events to project objectives.

9. *Project procurement management.* Procurement of necessary goods and services for the project is the logistical aspect of managing a job. It involves deciding what must be procured, issuing requests for bids or quotes, selecting vendors, administering contracts, and closing them when the job is finished.

The following are some examples of projects:

▶ Developing and introducing a new product
▶ Designing and implementing an information technology (IT) system
▶ Modernizing a factory
▶ Consolidating two manufacturing plants
▶ Designing and producing a brochure
▶ Executing an environmental clean-up of a contaminated site
▶ Building a shopping mall
▶ Rebuilding a town after a natural disaster
▶ Designing a business internship program for high school students
▶ Building a Wi-Fi system.

CHAPTER 2

Planning and Controlling Projects

The purpose of the project should be clearly defined. The management of a project requires proper planning and control of a project's completion time, budgetary resources, and desired results. Without proper planning and control, it is highly unlikely that the project will be completed within the deadline or with limited resources, or that the desired results will be achieved.

Key Questions to be Asked

In planning and controlling a project, the following questions should be asked:

Project Objective
- ▶ What are the desired results?
- ▶ What do we expect to achieve by undertaking this project?
- ▶ What problems are likely to be encountered?
- ▶ How will those problems be solved?

Time Considerations
- ▶ What is the magnitude of the project?
- ▶ Is it a large project or a small project?
- ▶ If it is a large project, how can it be divided into a series of shorter tasks?
- ▶ How long will it take to complete the project?
- ▶ What is the project's deadline?
- ▶ What are the consequences of not meeting the deadline or postponing the deadline?
- ▶ For longer projects, when should each phase of the project be completed?

Financial Considerations

▶ What is the project's budget?
▶ What are the major expense categories?
▶ Will capital expenditures be undertaken?
▶ How much of the budget should be allocated to planned expenses?
▶ How much of the budget should be allocated to unexpected expenses and contingency planning?
▶ What are the consequences of going over or under budget?
▶ What resources, including human resources, are needed to complete the project?
▶ What tools and methods will be used to ensure that the project is within budget?

Management

▶ What is my responsibility?
▶ Who will be on my project team?
▶ What is the responsibility of each team member?
▶ Who will manage and coordinate the various activities in a project and ensure that they are proceeding as planned and that the project will be completed before the deadline?
▶ Who will monitor that the project is proceeding as planned and within budget?
▶ How will deviations be identified and corrected for?
▶ Interim Analysis
▶ Are the intermediate results consistent with the final desired results?
▶ Is the project arriving at the desired results for each major step along its completion path?
▶ How will the pace be accelerated if your team falls behind schedule?
▶ How will costs be reduced if actual costs begin exceeding the budget?
▶ If problems are developing, what actions will be taken to correct them?

Final Report

▶ How will the results of the project be documented?
▶ What type of final report will be prepared and by whom? For whom?

To successfully complete the project, the project manager must have a clear understanding of the desired results and how these results will satisfy the needs of the end-user.

To successfully complete the project, the project manager must have a clear understanding of the answers to these questions and of how the desired results satisfy the needs of the end-user.

Project managers should assume a leadership position. Their aim should be not only to supervise but more importantly to coordinate the efforts of the team members. This often requires direct involvement in the major phases of the task so that the team works together, budgets do not show significant variances, schedules are kept, and deadlines are met.

A schedule of work should be prepared for outlining responsibilities. Everything should be written down. Checklists should be used to ensure that all team members know their responsibilities and deadlines. Team members sometimes work on several projects simultaneously. Under these conditions, there may be conflicts among priorities, especially if' they are working under different project managers. To minimize such conflicts, team members should be asked to let project managers know in advance about scheduling conflicts. Team members may then be reassigned to different tasks.

Team members should be given detailed instructions, and participation should be encouraged from the beginning. Their input should be solicited. Let the members propose solutions and assist in implementation. Active participation will motivate the project team, and when the ideas are good, the entire project benefits.

Conducting the Initial Meeting

Before starting the project, the project manager should meet with the team to set a positive tone and define the project's purpose. The meeting can help avoid misunderstandings and save time and effort later. It also clarifies the nature of the assignment, as well as the authority and responsibility of each individual.

Meetings should then be scheduled at regular intervals, but limited in time and frequency. If the project team spends all its time in meetings, not much else will be accomplished. At the same time, it is important to get together to review progress, resolve problems, and ensure adherence to budgets and schedules.

At the initial meeting, each team member should identify the problems he or she anticipates in working on the project. A list should of anticipated problems should be prepared and team members should generate solutions. If additional data is needed, a discussion should be started regarding who will research the data and from what sources. How will this information be verified? What if the data are inaccurate, obsolete, or misinterpreted? Be sure to consider how much time it will take to gather and check additional data or to conduct research.

A list of initial tasks should be prepared and assigned to appropriate individuals. Whenever possible, let the team members volunteer; they are likely to be more motivated if they define their own roles. The entire team should gain an understanding of the scope of the entire project at the initial meeting.

For all major phases of the project, prepare an *initial schedule*. For each phase, as well as for the overall project, establish the anticipated start and completion dates. Some phases, of course, may overlap. Subgroups of the team may be working independently and the work of one subgroup may not depend on the work of another subgroup. Nonlinearity in a project and its overlapping phases offer tremendous flexibility in scheduling activities.

While deadlines should be established in the initial schedule, maintaining flexibility is also important. It is highly unlikely that everything will happen according to schedule. Furthermore, as the team starts its work, the members will gain a better understanding of the problems, and the schedule and budget may have to be modified.

An initial financial budget should be prepared for each phase of the project. The initial budget should be prepared after considering human, financial, and information resources. For capital expenditures, consider both purchasing and leasing, as appropriate. Variance analysis should be conducted at the end of each phase by comparing the actual to budget Exhibits for costs, time, and productivity. This allows you to monitor actual expenditures and time, and to take corrective action, if necessary, to keep the project within budget.

Assembling the Project Team

The project team is a major determinant of the success or failure of a project. As the team increases in size, its diversity increases, managing the tasks becomes more difficult and complex, and the potential for conflict increases. There might be misunderstandings in communication. Different individuals have different motives and goals.

Team Assignment

As a project manager, you may or may not have control over the staff members assigned to the project team. If a team is being imposed, you should communicate with senior management and request that they allow your involvement in the selection process. For example, you could give them a list of individuals with whom you have worked successfully in the past. Emphasize the importance of having a cohesive project team and that such a team is critical to the project's success.

Of course, sometimes it just is not possible to put together a team of your choice and you have to do the best with those you are given. These individuals may be perfectly capable of doing the job. Alternatively, they may have been assigned to this project simply because they were available. It is also possible that these individuals were assigned because of their interest or talent. In any event, you should give each individual a chance to do the best possible work, and you may find yourself pleasantly surprised.

It is important to inspire and motivate team members. Your aim should be to help team members understand how the success of the project will affect their individual success. It is common for individuals to place top priority on self-gain, so ensuring that team members anticipate personal success ensures their commitment to the project. You need to specifically identify the benefits to the team members to motivate them and to focus their energies on the project. An ideal team member understands the desired results and is committed to making it happen.

Job Assignment

It is generally best to break a large project into several phases and each phase into distinct tasks. Each team member should then be assigned the responsibility of executing one or more of those tasks, which should not be highly structured. To motivate team members, assign them the responsibility for a given job and let them approach it the way they believe is best. This, of course, does not mean that you should not supervise them or give them guidance. Coordinate the activities and make sure the team members understand the goals and aims of the task. However, by providing team members with responsibility for certain tasks, you give them an incentive to put in their best efforts. This also lets them know that you trust them and that you have confidence in their abilities.

Delegating Duties

If you are too assertive and too controlling, you may stifle the freedom of your project team and impede its creativity. An effective project manager knows how to delegate the work. You should not insist that the project be done your way. Your role should be to monitor the team's work and coordinate its efforts, while watching the budget and the time schedule of each phase of the project. Of course, you should be available to help your team members, especially if they come to you with a problem.

Conflict Resolution

Conflicts sometimes develop among team members or groups of team members. For example, individuals may differ as to how to approach the project or solve a problem, or groups may compete for credit for some work. As the project manager, your aim is to resolve conflicts and to make sure these conflicts do not destroy the progress of the project. Emphasize to your team that the success of the project is more important than the success of any individual. Stress that everyone benefits from the project's success and everyone loses from its failure.

Self-Directed Work Teams

The self-directed team structure is an alternate to the traditional team structure and has become very popular recently. A *self-directed team* is a group of well-trained workers with full responsibility for completing a well-defined segment of work. This segment of work may be the entire finished product or an intermediate part of the whole. Every member of the team shares equal responsibility for the entire segment of work. Conceptually, self-directed teams are the opposite of traditional teams that work in an assembly-line manner. In an assembly line, each worker assumes responsibility for only a narrow technical function. In self-directed teams, each worker is equally responsible for the entire segment. This, of course, requires that the team members receive extensive training in administrative, technical, and interpersonal skills to maintain a self-managing group. Self-directed teams have many more resources available to them compared with traditional teams.

Traditional teams assign a narrow function to each member. Since a large number of people contribute to the finished product, individual workers see little relationship between their efforts and the finished product. This often leads to apathy and alienation. All members in self-directed teams receive extensive cross-training, and they share in both the challenging as well as the routine activities for their segment of work.

Obtaining Senior Management Support

Obtaining the cooperation of senior management is essential. Senior management's involvement and attitude toward projects differ from company to company and from person to person. Senior management might be very supportive of the project or may hardly care at all about it. Senior management's attitudes may be classified as follows:

- ▶ "It is your project. You have to solve your own problems. I don't want to be bothered until it is completed."
- ▶ "I would be happy to work with you and resolve any problem you encounter."
- ▶ "Although I would like to help, there is nothing I can do. You will have to resolve this problem on your own."
- ▶ "Keep me apprised of the situation and any problems you encounter. I want to be informed of everything."

Regardless of senior management's attitude, you should be prepared to complete the project without any help. Frequently, you will have no choice but to do the best you can with limited or available resources.

Developing a Feasible Budget

The budgeting process may be a source of confusion and frustration for many project managers. There may be a great deal of pressure to remain within the budget. A *budget* is simply an estimate of the sources and uses of cash and other resources. Since the budget is an estimate, it is unlikely that the final expenditures will be exactly equal to the budget.

Preparing the budget at a realistic level is important. Agreeing to an inadequate budget is unwise. While it may be convenient at the formation stage to reduce or minimize conflict, you and your project will ultimately suffer. You will be expected to explain unfavorable variances to senior management. Moreover, you will likely receive a very negative response when your project goes over budget.

The budget should always be developed by the project manager. It is unrealistic to work with an imposed budget. The project manager is generally in the best position to estimate what the project should cost and is therefore responsible for explaining any resulting variances. Accordingly, you should always insist on developing your own budget and should not settle for an inadequate budget simply to minimize conflict at the outset. Otherwise, both you and your project will suffer in the long run.

Project budgets are typically more difficult to prepare and adjust than departmental budgets. Projects typically consist of nonroutine activities. Departmental budgets are generally prepared annually and are often revised quarterly or semiannually. In contrast, project budgets are devised for the life of the project and are not related to a fiscal year. Revisions to project budgets are uncommon in the absence of a mistake in the original budget or a major change in the scope of the project. Unfavorable variances in a project are typically noticed more readily than unfavorable variances in a departmental budget. At the departmental level, variances are often accepted as being inevitable, but similar variances in a project are often frowned upon. In general, a project manager is typically held to a higher level of accountability than a department manager.

The major expense in most projects is likely to be for human resources. When estimating labor expense, consider both the labor hours and the skill levels needed to complete each phase of the project. Multiplying the hours by the labor rate at each level will give the total labor cost.

Also for each phase of the project, prepare a detailed budget listing the materials, supplies, and equipment requirements, which may vary widely. Some projects consist essentially of administrative tasks and do not require any special materials or supplies. Other projects may require considerable expenditures on property, plant, or equipment.

Fixed and variable overhead is another major category of expenses for most projects. Companies differ in how they allocate fixed overhead, but it is usually by a formula. Overhead may be allocated based on labor hours, labor cost, machine hours, square feet, etc. Variable overhead is allocated to the project like other project-specific expenses. In general, overhead is more likely to be allocated for longer-term projects. For shorter-term projects, senior management may decide not to allocate overhead expenses. It is essential to identify significant variances from budgeted amounts. Most companies require formal variance analysis at the end of the project. You should do a variance analysis at each phase of the project and take corrective action, if needed. If a phase is long, consider doing monthly variance analyses. All significant variances, whether favorable or unfavorable, should be investigated.

If actual expenses exceed budgeted expenses, investigate the cause. Budgets are closely tied to work schedules. Certain phases might be taking longer than estimated. You may have no choice but to demand more work from your team members. Also, your original assumptions and estimates might be wrong, or a significant change might have occurred in the scope of the project. You may need to request senior management to revise the project budget. It is sometimes possible to absorb unfavorable variances from one phase into the next phase. Your personal involvement in future phases of the project might also enhance productivity. You may also need to initiate budgetary controls to curb spending.

It is important to investigate *all* significant variances, not just the unfavorable ones. Sometimes expenses turn out to be less than budgeted. Examine why you are under budget. Is your team more productive than anticipated? Was there a significant decline in the price of materials, supplies, or equipment? Were your original estimates inaccurate? Is quality being sacrificed in any way to obtain cost savings? Do you expect to incur expenses in later phases that might wipe out any savings from the earlier stages?

Detailed Time-Schedule Preparation

Prepare a schedule for each phase of the project. You will be unable to complete your project on time without planning and controlling the time budget. Even a small delay in one phase of a project can have a significant effect on the overall completion time. Many tasks in a project are interdependent. A small isolated delay may not be a problem, however, when activities are interdependent, a small delay might throw off the entire schedule.

The schedule should be reasonable and realistic. Some projects are plagued by delays. If you have been unable to complete the initial phases on time, it is unlikely that you will complete the project on time. An effective project manager knows how to set up a realistic time budget and how to follow through on the budget. Time-management skills are essential characteristics of a good project manager.

When planning the initial schedule, budget a little slack. But keep in mind project deadlines are often imposed and you may have no choice but to work within the imposed guidelines. Sometimes a delay in one phase of the project simply has to be overcome in a later phase.

As the project manager, you are responsible for staying on schedule and meeting the deadline. It does not matter what caused the delay. You are personally responsible for controlling the activities, monitoring progress, anticipating problems, and taking corrective actions before delays cause you to miss the final project deadline.

Although your goal should be to meet the project deadline, it is unwise to let the quality of the project suffer. Your final results should be accurate and of high quality, even if it means requesting an extension. You should try, of course, to work faster, put in overtime, or modify your original plan in order to meet the deadline. Ultimately, if the trade-off is between meeting the deadline or doing quality work, the project's quality should take top priority.

Project Scorecard

A project scorecard measures the characteristics of the deliverables produced by a project. It also measures the progress of the internal project processes that create those deliverables.

Exhibit 2 provides the types of metrics that could be reported. This list is *not* exhaustive by any means but may help provide additional ideas for you.

Exhibit 2: Project Scorecard Metrics

BALANCE CATEGORY	SAMPLE METRICS
Cost	Actual cost vs. budget (variance) for project, for phase, for activity, etc.
	Total support costs for x months after solution is completed
	Total labor costs vs. nonlabor (vs. budget)
	Total cost of employees vs. cost of contract vs. cost of consultant (vs. budget)
	Cost associated with building components for reuse
	Total cost per transaction
	Ideas for cost reductions implemented and cost savings realized
Effort	Actual effort vs. budget (variance)
	Amount of project manager time vs. overall effort hours
Duration	Actual duration vs. budget (variance)
Productivity *Difficult to measure accurately unless function points are counted*	Effort hours per unit of work/function point
	Work units/function points produced per effort hour
	Effort hours reduced from standard project processes
	Effort hours saved through reuse of previous deliverables, models, components, etc.
	Number of process improvement ideas implemented
	Number of hours/dollars saved from process improvements
Quality of deliverables	Percentage of deliverables going through quality reviews
	Percentage of deliverable reviews resulting in acceptance the first time
	Number of defects discovered after initial acceptance
	Percentage of deliverables that comply 100 percent with organization standards
	Percentage of deliverables that comply with organization architectural standards
	Number of customer change requests to revise scope
	Number of hours of rework to previously completed deliverables
	Number of best practices identified and applied on the project
	Number of successfully mitigated risks

BALANCE CATEGORY	SAMPLE METRICS
Customer satisfaction with deliverables	Overall customer satisfaction (survey) with deliverables in terms of: Reliability Minimal defects Usability Response time Ease of use Availability Flexibility Intuitiveness Security Meets customer needs Understandable User documentation Application response time (calculated by the system) Number of approved business requirements satisfied by the project
Customer satisfaction with project team	Overall customer satisfaction (survey) with the project team in terms of: Responsiveness Competence Accessibility Courteousness Communication skills Credibility Knowledge of the customer Reliability/following through on commitments Professionalism Training provided Overall customer satisfaction Turnaround time required to answer customer queries and problems Average time required to resolve issues Number of scope change requests satisfied within original project budget and duration

BALANCE CATEGORY	SAMPLE METRICS
Business value	Overall customer satisfaction (survey) with deliverables in terms of:
	Reliability
	Minimal defects
	Usability
	Response time
	Ease of use
	Availability
	Flexibility
	Intuitiveness
	Security
	Meets customer needs
	Understandable
	User documentation
	Application response time (calculated by the system)
	Number of approved business requirements satisfied by the project

Terminating the Project

The fourth and final phase of the project life cycle is terminating the project. It starts after the project work has been completed and includes various actions to properly close out the project.

The purpose of properly terminating a project is to learn from the experience gained on the project in order to improve performance on future projects. Therefore, the activities associated with terminating the project should be identified and included in the project's *baseline plan*—they should not be done merely as spontaneous afterthoughts. These activities might include organizing and filing project documents, receiving and making final payments, and conducting post-project evaluation meetings within both the contractor's and the customer's organization.

The termination phase starts when performance of the project is completed and the result is accepted by the customer. In some situations, this might be a somewhat formal event in which an automated system satisfies a set of criteria or passes tests that were stated in the contract. Other projects, such as a weekend of homecoming activities at a university, are completed merely with the passage of time.

CHAPTER 3

Project Management Concepts and Process

A *project* is an endeavor to accomplish a specific objective through effectively utilizing resources in order to complete a unique set of interrelated tasks. The following attributes help define a project:

▶ A project has a well-defined objective—an expected result or product. The objective of a project is usually defined in terms of *scope, schedule,* and *cost.* For example, the objective of a project might be to introduce to the market— in 10 months and within a budget of $400,000—a new food preparation appliance that meets certain predefined performance specifications. The project team must complete a scope statement for developing a common understanding of the project scope among stakeholders. This lists project deliverables – summary level sub-products, whose full and satisfactory delivery marks the completion of the project. Furthermore, it is expected that the work scope will be accomplished in a quality manner and to the *customer's satisfaction.*

▶ A project is carried out through a series of *interdependent tasks*— that is, a number of nonrepetitive tasks that need to be accomplished in a certain sequence in order to achieve the project objective.

▶ A project utilizes various *resources* to carry out the tasks. Such resources can include different people, organizations, equipment, materials, and facilities. For example, a wedding is a project that may involve resources such as a caterer, a florist, a limousine, and a reception hall.

▶ A project has a *specific time frame*, or finite life span. It has a start time and a date by which the objective must be accomplished. For example, the refurbishing of an elementary school might have to be completed between June 20 and August 20.

▶ A project may be a *unique occurrence* or *one-time endeavor*. Some projects—like designing and building a space station on Mars—are unique because they have never before been attempted. Other projects, such as developing a new product, building a house, or planning a wedding, are unique because of the customization required. For example, a wedding can be a simple informal occasion, with a few friends in a chapel, or a spectacular event staged for a royal family.

▶ A project has a stakeholder. The *stakeholder* (or customer) is the entity that provides the funds necessary to accomplish the project—it can be a person, an organization, or a group of two or more people or organizations. When a contractor builds a customized home for a couple, the couple is the stakeholder funding the project. When a company receives funds from the government to develop a robotic device for handling radioactive material, the stakeholder is the government agency. When a company provides funds for a team of its employees to upgrade the firm's management information system, the term *stakeholder* takes on a broader definition, including not only the project funder (the company's management) but also other stakeholders, such as the people who will be the end users of the information system. The person managing the project and the project team must successfully accomplish the project objective to satisfy the stakeholder(s).

▶ Finally, a project involves a *degree of uncertainty*. Before a project is started, a plan is prepared based on certain assumptions and estimates. It is important to document these assumptions, since they will influence the development of the project budget, schedule, and work scope. A project is based on a unique set of tasks and estimates of how long each task should take, various resources and assumptions about the availability and capability of those resources, and estimates of the costs associated with the resources. This combination of assumptions and estimates causes a degree of uncertainty as to whether the project objective can or will be completely accomplished by deadline. For example, the project scope may be accomplished by the target date, but the final cost may be much higher than anticipated because of low initial estimates for the cost of certain resources. As the project proceeds, some of the assumptions will be refined or replaced with factual information. For example, once the conceptual design of a company's annual report is finalized, the amount of time and effort needed to complete the detailed design and printing can be better estimated.

The successful accomplishment of the project objective is usually constrained by four factors: *scope, cost, schedule,* and *customer satisfaction.*

The scope of a project—also known as the *project scope,* or *work scope*—is all the work that must be done in order to ensure that the customer is completely satisfied and that the deliverables (the tangible product or items to be provided) *meet the requirements or acceptance criteria agreed upon at the onset of the project.* For example, a project scope might include all of the work involved in clearing the land, building a house, and landscaping to the specifications agreed upon by the contractor and the buyer. The customer expects the work scope to be accomplished in a quality manner. For example, in a house-building project, the customer expects the workmanship to be of the highest quality. Completing the work scope but leaving windows that are difficult to open and close, faucets that leak, or a landscape full of rocks will result in an unsatisfied customer.

The *cost* of a project is the amount the customer has agreed to pay for acceptable project deliverables. The project cost is based on a budget that is determined by cost estimates of all necessary resources for completing the project. It might include the salaries of people who will work on the project, materials and supplies, equipment or facility rentals, and the fees of subcontractors or consultants who will perform some of the project tasks. For example, if the project is a wedding, some of the budgeted items might include flowers, wedding gown, tuxedo, caterer, cake, limousine rental, photographer, and so on.

The *schedule* for a project is the timetable that specifies when each activity should start and finish. The project objective usually states the time by which the project scope must be completed, which is typically a specific date agreed upon by the customer and the individual or organization performing the work. It might be the date when a town's centennial celebration will take place or the date by which you want to complete the addition of a family room to your home.

The objective of any project is to complete the scope within budget, by a certain date, and to the customer's satisfaction. To help assure the achievement of this objective, *it is important to develop a plan before the start of the project; this plan should include all the work tasks, associated costs, and estimates of the time necessary to complete them.* The lack of such a plan increases the risk of failing to accomplish the full project scope within budget and on schedule.

Once a project is started, unforeseen circumstances may arise that jeopardize the achievement of the project objective with respect to scope, cost, or schedule. Here are a few examples:

▶ The cost of some of the materials may be higher than originally estimated.
▶ Inclement weather may cause a delay.

▶ Additional redesign and modifications to a sophisticated piece of automated machinery may be required to get it to meet the performance specifications.

The challenge to the project manager is to prevent, anticipate, and/or overcome such circumstances in order to complete the project scope on schedule, within budget, and to the customer's satisfaction. *Good planning and communication* are essential to prevent problems from occurring and to minimize the impact of these problems on the achievement of the project objective should they occur. The project manager needs to be proactive in planning and communicating and should demonstrate strong leadership toward the project team in helping them to accomplish the project objective.

Ultimately, the responsibility of the project manager is to make sure the customer is satisfied. This goes beyond just completing the project scope within budget and on schedule or asking the customer at the end of the project if he or she is satisfied. It requires ongoing communication with the customer to keep the customer informed and to determine whether expectations have changed. Regularly scheduled meetings or progress reports, frequent phone discussions, and email are examples of ways to maintain such communications. Customer satisfaction means involving the customer as a partner in the successful outcome of the project by allowing them to actively participate in many aspects of the project. The project manager must be aware of the degree of customer satisfaction throughout the project. By maintaining regular communication with the customer, the project manager demonstrates to the customer that he or she is genuinely concerned with the expectations of the customer which may prevent unpleasant surprises later.

Project Life Cycle

In project management, the sequence of project phases and phase gates is often referred to as *project life cycle*. Exhibit 3 shows the four phases of the *project life cycle* and the relative amount of effort and time devoted to each phase. As the project moves through its life cycle, different organizations, individuals, and resources play dominant roles.

Exhibit 3: Project Life Cycle

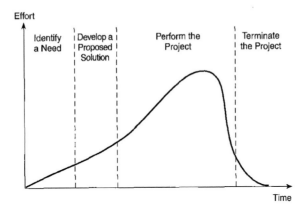

Projects are "born" when a need is identified by the *customer*—the people or the organization willing to provide funds to have the need satisfied. For example, for a growing family, the need may be for a larger house, whereas for a company, the problem may be a high scrap rate from its manufacturing process that makes its costs higher and production times longer than those of its competitors. The customer first must identify the need or problem. Sometimes the problem is identified quickly, as in the case of a disaster such as an earthquake or explosion. In other situations, it may take months for a customer to clearly identify a need, gather data on the problem, and define certain requirements that must be met by the person, project team, or contractor who will solve the problem.

This first *phase* of the project life cycle involves the identification of a need, problem, or opportunity. Once the need has been identified, the customer may request proposals from individuals, project teams, or organizations (contractors) to address the identified need or solve the problem. The needs and requirements are usually written up by the customer in a document called a *request for proposal (RFP)*. Through the RFP, the customer asks individuals or contractors to submit proposals on how they might solve the problem, along with the associated cost and schedule. A couple who needs a new house may spend time identifying requirements for the house—size, style, number of rooms, location, maximum amount they want to spend, and date by which they would like to move in. They may then write down these requirements and ask several contractors to provide house plans and cost estimates. A company that has identified a need to upgrade its computer system might document its requirements in an RFP and send it to several computer consulting firms. Not all situations involve a formal RFP, however. Needs are often defined informally during a meeting or discussion among a group of individuals.

Some of the individuals may then volunteer or be requested to prepare a proposal to determine whether a project should be undertaken to address the need. Such a scenario might be played out when the management of a hospital wants to establish an on-site daycare center for the children of its employees. The management team or a specific manager may write down the requirements in a document and give it to an internal project team, who in turn will submit a proposal for how to establish the center. In this case, the contractor is the hospital's own internal project team, and the customer is the hospital's manager or, possibly, board of directors. It is important to accurately define the precise need. For example, is the need to provide an on-site daycare center, or is it merely to provide child care hospital employees? In other words, is it necessary for the daycare to be "on-site"?

The *second phase* of the project life cycle is the development of a proposed solution to the need or problem. This phase results in the submission of a *proposal* to the customer by one or more individuals or organizations (contractors) who would like to be hired by the customer for paid implementation of the proposed solution. In this phase, the contractor's effort becomes dominant. Contractors interested in responding to the RFP may spend several weeks developing approaches to solving the problem, estimating the types and amounts of resources that would be needed, and estimating the time it would take to design and implement the proposed solution. Each contractor documents this information in a written proposal. All of the contractors then submit their proposals to the customer. For example, several contractors may submit proposals to a customer to develop and implement an automated invoicing and collection system. After the customer evaluates the submissions and selects the winning proposal, the customer and the winning contractor negotiate and sign a *contract* (agreement). In many situations, a request for proposal may not involve soliciting competitive proposals from external contractors. A company's own internal project team may develop a proposal in response to a management-defined need or request. In this case, the project would be performed by the company's own employees rather than an external contractor.

The *third phase* of the project life cycle is the implementation of the proposed solution. This phase begins after the customer decides which of the proposed solutions will best fulfill their need and an agreement is reached between the customer and the chosen individual or contractor. This phase, sometimes referred to as performing the project, involves detailed planning for the project and implementation of that plan to accomplish the project objective. During the course of the project, different types of resources will be utilized. For example, if the project is to design and construct an office building, the project effort might first involve a few architects and engineers who can draw up the building plans. Then, as construction gets under way, the resources needed will substantially increase to include steelworkers, carpenters, electricians, painters, and the like. The project will wind down after the building is finished, and a smaller number of different workers will finish up the landscaping and final interior touches. Once this final phase is completed, if the customer is satisfied that the full scope of work was completed on time, within budget, and in a quality manner, then the project can be said to be completed and the goal accomplished. For example, the third phase is complete when a contractor has completed the design and installation of a customized automation system that satisfactorily passes performance tests and is accepted by the customer or when an internal project team within a company has completed a project, in response to a management request, which consolidated two of its facilities into one.

The *final phase* of the project life cycle is terminating the project. When a project is completed, certain close-out activities need to be performed, such as confirming that all deliverables have been received and accepted by the customer, all payments have been collected, and all invoices have been paid. An important task during this phase is evaluating performance of the project team in order to learn what could be improved if a similar project were to be carried out in the future. This phase should include obtaining feedback from the customer to determine the level of the customer's satisfaction and whether the project met the customer's expectations. Also, recommendations and feedback from the project team will help improve performance of similar projects in the future.

Project life cycles vary in length from a few weeks to several years, depending on the content, complexity, and magnitude of the project. What's more, not all projects formally go through all four phases of the project life cycle. If a group of community volunteers decides that they want to use their own time, talents, and resources to organize a food drive for the homeless, they may get right into phase three—planning the event and carrying it out. The first two phases of the life cycle would not be relevant to such a project. Likewise, if a company's general manager determines that changing the layout of equipment in the factory will increase efficiency, he or she might simply instruct the manufacturing manager to initiate such a project and to implement it using the company's own people. In this case, there would be no written request for proposal from external contractors.

In other situations, such as a home remodeling project for which a contractor will likely be hired, a customer may go through the first two phases of the project life cycle in a less structured, more informal manner. He or she may not write down all of the requirements or ask several contractors for estimates. Rather, they may call a specific contractor who has been recommended by a friend or neighbor, explain what the job is, and ask that contractor to provide some sketches and a cost estimate.

In general, the project life cycle is followed in a more formal and structured manner when a project is conducted in a business setting. It tends to be less formal when a project is carried out by a private individual or volunteers.

Types of Contracts

Contract type is an important consideration. Different types of contracts can be used in different situations. Two broad categories of contracts are fixed price or lump sum, cost reimbursable, and unit price.

Fixed price or *lump sum contracts* involve a fixed total price for a well-defined product or service. The buyer incurs little risk in this situation. For example, a company could award a fixed price contract to purchase 100 laser printers with a certain print resolution and print speed to be delivered to one location within two months. In this example, the product and delivery date are well defined. Fixed price contracts may also include incentives for meeting or exceeding selected project objectives. For example, the contract could include an incentive fee paid if the laser printers are delivered within one month. A *firm-fixed price contract* has the least amount of risk for the consumer, followed by a *fixed price incentive contract*.

Cost reimbursable contracts involve payment to the seller for direct and indirect actual costs. Direct costs are costs that are related to a project and can be traced back in a cost-effective way. Indirect costs are costs related to the project that cannot be traced back in a cost-effective way. For example, the salaries for people working directly on a project and hardware or software purchased for a specific project are direct costs, while the cost of providing a work space with electricity, a cafeteria, and the like are indirect costs. Indirect costs are often calculated as a percentage of direct costs. Cost reimbursable contracts often include fees such as a profit percentage or incentives for meeting or exceeding selected project objectives. These contracts are often used for projects that include providing goods and services that involve new technologies. The consumer absorbs more of the risk with cost reimbursable contracts than they do with fixed price contracts.

The Project Management Process

Succinctly, the project management process means *planning the work* and then *working the plan*. A coaching staff may spend hours preparing unique plans for a game, then the team executes the plans to meet the objective and the result—victory. Similarly, project management involves a process of first *establishing a plan* and then *implementing that plan* to accomplish the project objective.

The front-end effort in managing a project must be focused on establishing a baseline plan that provides a roadmap for how the project scope will be accomplished on time and within budget. This planning effort includes the following:

1. *Clearly define the project objective.* The goal must be defined in a way that is agreed upon by the customer and the individual or organization that will perform the project.

2. *Divide and subdivide the project scope into major "pieces," or* **work packages**. Although major projects may seem overwhelming when viewed as a whole, one way to conquer even the most monumental endeavor is to break it down. A **work breakdown structure** *(WBS)* is a hierarchical tree of work elements or items accomplished or produced by the project team during the project. The work breakdown structure usually identifies the organization or individual responsible for each work package. Exhibit 4 is an example of a work breakdown structure (WBS). Chapter 4 discusses the WBS.

Exhibit 4: Work breakdown structure (WBS)

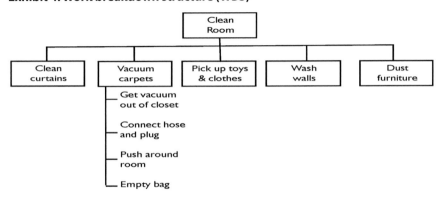

3. *Define the specific activities that need to be performed for each work package in order to accomplish the project objective.* In Exhibit 4, the work package, Vacuum carpets involves many smaller specific activities involved in the broader task of vacuuming the carpet.

4. *Graphically portray the activities in the form of a* **network diagram.** This type of diagram shows the necessary sequence and interdependencies of activities to achieve the project objective. (Network diagrams will be discussed further in Chapter 5.)

5. *Make a* **time estimate** *for how long it will take to complete each activity.* It is also necessary to determine which types of resources and how many of each resource are needed for each activity to be completed within the estimated duration.

6. *Make a cost estimate for each activity.* The cost is based on the types and quantities of resources required for each activity.

7. *Calculate a project schedule and budget to determine whether the project can be completed within the required time, with the allotted funds, and with the available resources.* If it is determined that the project cannot be accomplished within the limitations, adjustments must be made to the project scope, activity time estimates, or resource assignments until an achievable, realistic *baseline plan* (a roadmap for accomplishing the project scope on time and within budget) can be established. Exhibit 5 shows an example of a project schedule, and Exhibit 6 illustrates a project budget. (These will be covered in Chapters 5 and 7.)

Exhibit5: Network Diagram – Consumer Market Study Project

	ACTIVITY	RESPON.	DUR. ESTIM.	EARLIEST		LATEST		TOTAL SLACK	
				START	FINISH	START	FINISH		
1	Identify Target Consumers	Susan	3	0	3	−8	−5	−8	
2	Develop Draft Questionnaire	Susan	10	3	13	−5	5	−8	
3	Pilot-Test Questionnaire	Susan	20	13	33	5	25	−8	
4	Review Comments & Finalize Questionnaire	Susan	5	33	38	25	30	−8	
5	Prepare Mailing Labels	Steve	2	38	40	38	40	0	
6	Print Questionnaire	Steve	10	38	48	30	40	−8	
7	Develop Data Analysis Software	Andy	12	38	50	88	100	50	
8	Develop Software Test Data	Susan	2	38	40	98	100	60	
9	Mail Questionnaire & Get Responses	Steve	65	48	113	40	105	−8	
10	Test Software	Andy	5	50	55	100	105	50	
11	Input Response Data	Jim	7	113	120	105	112	−8	
12	Analyze Results	Jim	8	120	128	112	120	−8	
13	Prepare Report	Jim	10	128	138	120	130	−8	

Exhibit 6: Project Budget

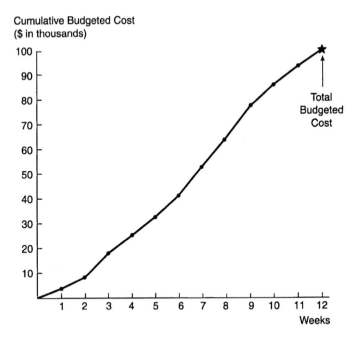

Planning determines what needs to be done, who will do it, how long it will take, and how much it will cost. The result of this effort is a baseline plan. Taking the time to develop a well thought out plan is critical to the successful accomplishment of any project. Many projects have overrun their budgets, missed their completion dates, or only partially met their requirements because there was no viable baseline plan before the project was started.

The baseline plan for a project can be displayed in graphical or tabular format for each time period (i.e. week, month) from the start of the project to its completion. (Plans are discussed and illustrated in Chapter 3.) Information should include:

▶ The start and completion dates for each activity
▶ The amounts of the various resources that will be needed during each time period
▶ The budget for each time period, as well as the cumulative budget from the start of the project through each time period

Once a baseline plan has been established, it must be implemented. This involves performing the work according to the plan and controlling the work so that the project scope is achieved within the budget and schedule, to the customer's satisfaction.

Once the project starts, it is necessary to monitor progress to ensure that everything is going according to plan. At this stage, the project management process involves measuring actual progress and comparing it to planned progress. To measure actual progress, it is important to keep track of which activities have actually been started and/or completed, when they were started and/or completed, and how much money has been spent or committed. If at any time during the project comparison of actual progress to planned progress reveals that the project is behind schedule, overrunning the budget, or not meeting the technical specifications, corrective action must be taken to get the project back on track.

Before a decision is made to implement corrective action, it may be necessary to evaluate several alternative actions to make sure the corrective action will bring the project back within the scope, time, and budget constraints of the objective. Be aware, for instance, that adding resources to make up time and get back on schedule may result in overrunning the planned budget. If a project gets too far out of control, it may be difficult to achieve the project objective without sacrificing the scope, budget, schedule, quality, or all of the above.

The key to effective project control is measuring actual progress and comparing it to planned progress on a timely and regular basis and taking corrective action immediately, if necessary. Hoping that a problem will go away without corrective intervention is naïve and irresponsible. Based on actual progress, it is possible to forecast a schedule and budget for completion of the project. If these parameters are beyond the limits of the project objective, corrective actions need to be implemented at once.

Attempting to perform a project without first establishing a baseline plan is foolhardy. It is like starting a vacation without a roadmap, itinerary, and budget. You may land up in the middle of nowhere— out of money and out of time.

Benefits of Project Management

The ultimate benefit of implementing project management techniques is having a *satisfied stakeholder (customer)*—whether you are the customer of your own project, such as remodeling your basement, or a business (contractor) being paid by a customer to perform a project. Ultimately, in the close-out phase, the customer has the greatest influence on the quality, scope, time and cost of the project. Completing the full project scope in a quality manner, on time, and within budget provides a great feeling of satisfaction. For a contractor, it could lead to additional business from the same customer in the future or to business from new customers referred by previously satisfied customers.

CHAPTER 4

Using the Work Breakdown Structure to Plan a Project

Planning answers the questions "What must be done?," "How long will it take?," and "How much will it cost?" Planning the "What" is vital; projects frequently fail because a significant part of the work is forgotten. In addition, once tasks have been identified, the time and resource requirements must be determined. This is called *estimating*.

A major problem in project planning is determining how long tasks will take and what it will cost to do them. Inaccurate estimates are a leading cause of project failures, and missed cost targets are a common cause of stress and recrimination in project management.

The most useful tool for accomplishing all of these tasks is the *Work Breakdown Structure (WBS)*. The idea behind the WBS is simple: you can subdivide a complicated task into smaller tasks, until you reach a level that cannot be further subdivided. Decomposition is used in developing the WBS. A that point, it is usually easier to estimate how long the small task will take and how much it will cost to perform than it would have been to estimate these factors at higher levels.

Nevertheless, it is still no easy feat to estimate task durations for activities that have never been performed before. Because this is the typical situation in engineering hardware and software development projects, we might expect many of these estimates to be in error, and this seems to be demonstrated by experience. Still, the Work Breakdown Structure makes it easier to estimate knowledge tasks than any other tool we have.

A Simple Example

As an example, if I want to clean a room (see Exhibit 7), I might begin by picking up clothes, toys, and other things that have been dropped on the floor. I could use a vacuum cleaner to get dirt out of the carpet. I might wash the windows and wipe down the walls, then dust the furniture. All of these activities are *subtasks* performed to clean the room.

As for vacuuming the room, you might have to get the vacuum cleaner out of the closet, connect the hose, plug it in, push the vacuum cleaner around the room, empty the bag, and put the machine back in the closet. These are still smaller tasks to be performed in accomplishing the subtask called *vacuuming*. The diagram in Exhibit 7 shows how this might be portrayed in WBS format.

Exhibit 7: WBS Diagram to Clean a Room

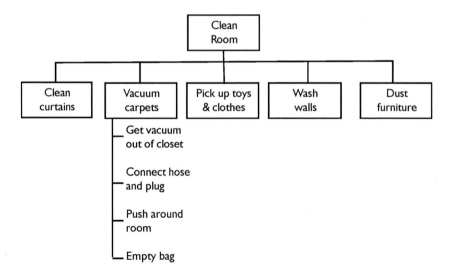

Note that we do not worry about the sequence in which work is performed when we do a WBS. That will be worked out when we develop a schedule. However, you will probably find yourself thinking sequentially, as it seems to be human nature to do so. The main idea of doing a WBS is to capture all of the tasks. So if you mind yourself and other members of your team thinking sequentially, don't be too concerned, but don't get hung up on trying to diagram the sequence or you will slow down the process of task identification.

The typical WBS has three to six levels, and these can be labeled as shown in Exhibit 8. It is, of course, possible to have projects that require a lot more levels. Twenty levels is considered to be the upper limit, and that is a huge project. Note that level 1 is called the *program level*. The difference between a program and a project is just one of degree.

Exhibit 8: WBS Level Names

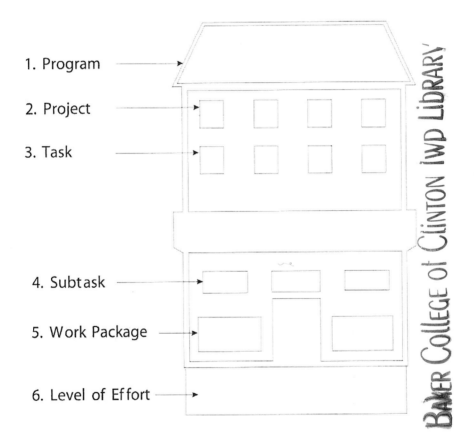

1. Program

2. Project

3. Task

4. Subtask

5. Work Package

6. Level of Effort

An example of a program is the development of an airplane. For example, the WBS for Boeing's 787 airplane program might have been drawn as shown in Exhibit 9. Notice that the engine, wing, and avionics are large enough jobs to be called projects in their own right. In fact, the program manager's job is to make sure that the projects are all properly integrated. The engine mounts on the wing, so, somewhere in the structure to develop the engine, there will be an activity called "Design wing mounts." And for the wing, there will be an activity called "Design engine mounts." If these are not coordinated properly, you will wind up with an engine that won't mount on the wing. The job of coordinating these is called *system integration*.

Exhibit 9 : Partial WBS for the 787 Development Program

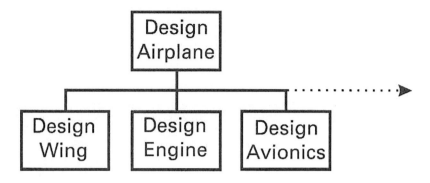

Guidelines for Developing the WBS

One important question in constructing a WBS is "When do you stop breaking down the work?" The general guideline is that you stop when you reach a point where either you can estimate time and cost to the desired degree of accuracy or the work will take an amount of time equal to the smallest units you want to schedule. If, for instance, you want to schedule to the nearest day, you break down the work to the point where tasks take about a day to perform. If you are going to schedule to the nearest hour, then you stop when task durations are in that range.

Remember the rule that the people who must do the work should participate in planning it? That applies here. Usually a core group identifies top-level parts of the WBS; those parts are further refined by other members of the team and then integrated to obtain the entire WBS.

One important point: the WBS should be developed before the schedule. In fact, the WBS is the device that ties the entire project together. It allows resources to be assigned and estimates of time and cost to be made and shows the scope of the job in graphic form. Later, as the project is tracked, the work can be identified as falling in a particular box in the WBS.

There are many software packages that print a WBS after schedule data have been entered. That is a nice feature, since it gives a graphically attractive WBS. It is important that the rough drawing be made prior to input in the scheduling software, though. The reason is quite simple: until everyone has agreed that all tasks have been identified, it is misleading to develop a schedule. You cannot be sure that the critical path identified by a partial schedule will be the same for the full schedule.

There are a number of approaches to developing the WBS. Ideally, you proceed top-down, following development of a good problem statement and mission statement. As previously mentioned, however, the mind does not always operate in such nice, linear fashion. As you develop the WBS, you may sometimes find that it helps to understand the job better. For that reason, about it is not necessary to be so strict about doing things in a specific order. You do what works best for you.

The WBS does not have to be symmetrical. That is, all paths need not be broken down to level 6 (or whatever level you stop at). Since the rule is to break work down to a level sufficient to achieve the estimating accuracy you desire, one path may take six levels, while another may need only three.

Uses of the WBS

The WBS is a good way to show the scope of a job. If you have ever given someone an estimate for project cost or time and seen the person's horrified look, you know that they are seeing the project in their mind as much simpler than it is. When you show a project in WBS for, it is clear to most individuals why the job costs so much. In fact, we see the experience of the planning group members themselves being overwhelmed by the complexity and magnitude of the WBS. If it impresses them, think of the impact on the outsider.

Assigning responsibility for tasks is another important use of the WBS. Each task to be performed should be assigned to a particular person who will be responsible for its completion. These assignments can then be listed on a separate form, often called a *responsibility chart* (see Exhibit 10).

Exhibit 10: Responsibility Chart

Linear Responsibility Chart				
Project:	Date Issued:		Sheet Number:	of
Manager:	Date Revised:		Revision No.	File: LRCFORM.61
Task Descriptions	Project Contributors			

CODES: 1 = ACTUAL RESPONSIBILITY; 2 = SUPPORT; 3 = MUST BE NOTIFIED; BLANK = NOT INVOLVED

Estimating Time, Costs, and Resources

Once the work is broken down, you can estimate how long it will take. But how? Suppose you ask how long it will take to sort a thoroughly shuffled standard deck of playing cards into numerical order by suit. How would you answer that question?

The most obvious way would be to try the task several times and get a felling for it. But if you didn't have a deck of cards handy, you would probably think about it, imagine how long it would take, and give an answer. People generally give answers ranging from two minutes to ten minutes. Tests indicate that about three minutes is average for most adults.

Suppose, however, the same task was given to a child about four or five years old. It might take a lot longer, since the child would not be that familiar with the sequence in which cards are ordered, and perhaps not yet even be that comfortable with counting. This leads to a very important conclusion: you cannot do a time or cost estimate without considering who will actually perform the task. Also, you must base the estimate on historical data or a mental model. Historical data are best.

Generally average times are used to plan projects. That is, if it takes three minutes on average for an adult to sort a deck of cards, three minutes would be a good estimate to use of how long it will take during execution of my project. Naturally, when using averages, some tasks will take longer than the time allowed and some will take less. Ultimately, however, they should all average out.

That is the idea, anyway. Parkinson's Law discredits this notion, however. Parkinson said that work always expands to fill the time allowed. That means that tasks may take longer than the estimated time, but they almost never take less. One reason is that when people find themselves with some time left, they tend to refine what they have done. Another is that people fear that if they turn work in early, they may be expected to do the task faster the next time or that they may be given more work to do.

This is a very important point: if people are penalized for performing better than the target, they will quit doing so. It is necessary to understand **variation**. If the same person sorts a deck of cards over and over, we know the sort times will vary. Sometimes it will take two minutes, while other times it will take four. The average may be three, but we may expect that half the time it will take three minutes or less and half the time it will take three minutes or more. Very seldom will it take *exactly* three minutes.

The same is true for *all* project tasks. The time it takes to perform them will vary, because of forces outside the person's control. The cards are shuffled differently every time. The person's attention is diverted by a loud noise outside. He drops a card while sorting. He gets tired. And so on.

Can you get rid of the variation? No way. Can you reduce it? Yes—through practice, by changing the process by which the work is done, and so on. But it is important to note that the variation will always be there, and you must recognize and accept it.

Consensual Estimating

Estimating can be hazardous. Guidelines for documenting estimates:

- ▶ Show the percent tolerance that is likely to apply.
- ▶ Tell how the estimate was made and what assumptions were used.
- ▶ Specify any factors that might affect the validity of the estimate (such as time—will the estimate still be valid in six months?).

In recent years, a new method of estimating knowledge work has been developed that seems to be better than older techniques. Rather than have every individual estimate task durations, the new method asks at least three people to estimate each activity in the project that they know something about. They do this without discussing their ideas with one another. They then meet to find out what they have put on paper. In a typical situation, there may be a range of times, such as, for example, ten days, twelve days, and thirty days, in which two of the estimates are close together, but one is very different. How do you handle the discrepancy?

The best approach is to discuss what each person was considering when he or she made the estimate. It may be that the person who put down thirty days was thinking about something that the other two had overlooked. Or, conversely, they may convince the thirty-day person that his number is way too high and get him to come down to a figure nearer their estimates. In any case, they try to arrive at a number that they all can support. This is called consensus.

There are three advantages to this approach. First, no one person is on the hook for the final number. Second, inexperienced people learn to estimate from those more experienced. Third, they are likely to collectively consider more issues than any one person would do working alone. For that reason, you are more likely to get an accurate estimate, although it is important to remember that it is still not exact.

Improving Estimating Ability

People cannot learn unless they receive feedback on this performance. If you went out every day and ran 100 yards, trying to improve your speed, but you never timed yourself, you would have no idea whether you were getting better or worse. You could be doing something that slowed you down, but you wouldn't know it. In the same way, if you estimate task durations but never record the actual time it takes to do the task, you are never going to get better at estimating. Furthermore, you have to track progress by recording times daily. If you record times once a week, it is guaranteed that you will be just guessing, and that won't be helpful.

CHAPTER 5

Project Scheduling

One of the primary features that distinguish project management from general management is the special attention to scheduling. A project is a *problem scheduled for solution*.

Project management involves planning and scheduling. *Project planning* includes all activities that result in a course of action for a project. Goals for the project must be set and their priorities established. Goals include resources to be committed, completion times, and activities. Areas of responsibility must be identified and assigned. Time and resource requirements to perform the work activities must be projected and budgeted. Project scheduling, compared to project planning, is more specific. Scheduling establishes time and sequences of the various phases of the project.

Project Scheduling Models

There are various methods for scheduling projects. Presented in this chapter are two popular scheduling models – *Gantt* charting and the *Program Evaluation and Review Technique (PERT)*. Both are schematic models, but the PERT also is a mathematical model.

Gantt Charts

A *Gantt chart* is a tool to monitor progress. Showing both planned and actual outcomes for each phase, a Gantt chart allows you to isolate and solve scheduling problems in a methodical manner. While the project as a whole might be overwhelming, a Gantt chart helps in managing a large project by breaking the project into a series of smaller phases. As each phase is completed, you can see if the final deadline is likely to be met. If you are behind schedule, you can attempt to get back on track by absorbing the delay in one phase by making it up in another phase. This tool should be used not only by the project manager, but by the entire team. Its use is most effective when everyone on the team uses it.

A Gantt chart may be constructed using several techniques involving different combinations of lines and symbols. The actual and planned beginning and ending points for each phase are plotted along a time line. The first phase is plotted at the top and the last phase is plotted at the bottom. Gantt charts may be constructed by hand or through computer software packages.

Exhibit 11 shows a Gantt chart of project planning. Project activities are listed down the page and time across the page. The heavy lines show how much of each activity has already been done. You can use this chart to visualize the progress and to adjust your project activities. As you can see, one of the strengths of project scheduling with Gantt charts is the simplicity of the schematic model.

Exhibit 11: Gantt Chart for Project SchedulinG

PROJECT PLANNING CHART

Project Number	01 - 650	Page	1 of 1
Project Name	Labor Cost Anaylsis Module	Prepared by	S. Doe
Project Leader	J. Flaherty	Date	12 / 8.

ACTIVITY		WEEK STARTING
No.	Name	11/17 11/24 12/1 12/8 12/15 12/22 12/29 1/5 1/12 1/19 1/26 2/2 2/9 2/16 2/23 3/2 3/9 3/16 3/23 3/30
1-1	Organize implementation team	
1-2	Prepare system support procedures	
1-3	Develop conversion plan	
1-4	Develop testing plan	
2-1	Prepare program specifications	
2-2	Revise system documentation	
2-3	Perform programming tasks	
3-1	System test	
4-1	Install system support procedures	
5-1	Acceptance test	
6-1	Conversion	

Program Evaluation and Review Technique (PERT)

Program Evaluation and Review Technique (PERT) is a useful management tool for planning, scheduling, costing, coordinating, and controlling complex projects such as (a) construction of buildings, (b) installation of computers, (c) assembly of a machine, (d) research and development activities, and (e) new product development.

Questions to be answered by PERT include:
▶ When will the project be finished?

▶ What is the probability that the project will be completed by any given time?

The PERT technique involves the diagrammatic representation of the sequence of activities comprising a project by means of a network. The network (1) visualizes all of the individual tasks (activities) to complete a given job or program; (2) points out interrelationships; and (3) consists of activities (represented by arrows) and events (represented by circles), as shown below.

1. *Arrows.* Arrows represent "tasks" or "activities," which are distinct segments of the project that consume time and resources.

2. *Nodes (circles).* Nodes symbolize "events," or milestone points in the project representing the completion of one or more activities and/or the initiation of one or more subsequent activities. An event is a point in time and does not consume any time in itself as does an activity.

Rules of Network Construction

Fundamental to PERT is the construction of a network. The rules for its construction follow:

Rule 1: Each arrow should represent only one activity.

Rule 2: The length of the arrow is determined only by convenience and clarity, and is not related to the time needed for that activity.

Rule 3: Each activity except the first must have an activity preceding it.

Rule 4: Each activity except the last must have an activity following it.

Rule 5: For any activity to begin, all preceding activities must be completed.

Example 1

Consider the activities, A, B, C, D, E, F, and G. The following network

is interpreted as:

1. Perform activity A.
2. Start B and C after A is performed. B and C can be performed concurrently.
3. Start D and E after B is completed.
4. Start F only after C *and* D are completed.
5. Start G only after E and F are completed.

> *Note:* It is evident that a network can represent the most complex relationship of activities conceivable and yet permit the tracking of all activities with little trouble.

An additional important rule must be noted:

Rule 6: No two activities can have the same origin and ending.

Example 2

Assume that we are to perform A and B concurrently. Because of Rule 6, the following network is illegal:

Because of Rule 4, the following network is illegal as it stands:

However, the problem can be resolved by what is called a *dummy activity* in the following way:

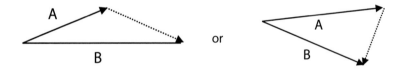

A dummy activity represents *no* work, but permits observance of Rule 4 and Rule 6.

In a real world situation, the estimates of completion times of activities will seldom be certain. To cope with the uncertainty in activity time estimates, the PERT proceeds by estimating three possible duration times for each activity. As shown in Exhibit 12, the numbers appearing on the arrows represent these three time estimates for activities needed to complete the various events. These time estimates are:

▶ The most optimistic time, labeled a
▶ The most likely time, m
▶ The most pessimistic time, b

Exhibit 12: Network Diagram

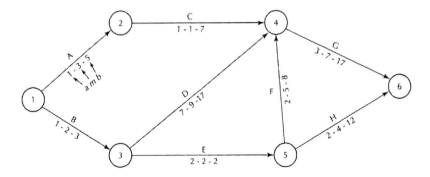

For example, the optimistic time for completing activity H is 2 days, the most likely time is 4 days, but the pessimistic time is 12 days. The next step is to calculate an expected time, which is determined as follows:

$$t_e \text{ (expected time)} = (a + 4m + b) / 6$$

For example, for activity H, the expected time is

$$(2 + 4(4) + 12) / 6 = 30 / 6 = 5 \text{ days}$$

Note that this formula is based on the assumption that the uncertain activity times are best described by a *beta probability distribution*. This distribution assumption, which was judged to be reasonable by the developers of PERT, provides the time distribution for activity H as shown in Exhibit 13.

Exhibit 13: Activity Time Distribution for Activity H

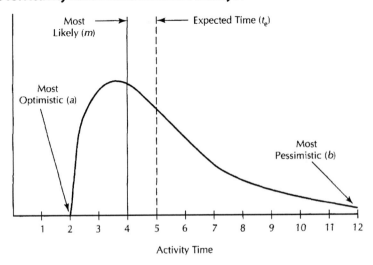

As a measure of variation (uncertainty) about the expected time, the standard deviation is calculated as follows:

$$\sigma = (b - a) / 6$$

For example, the standard deviation of completion time for activity H is:

$$\sigma \qquad = (12 - 2) / 6 = 10 / 6 = 1.67 \text{ days}$$

Note: This formula is based on the notion that a standard deviation is approximately 1/6 of the difference between the extreme values of the distribution.

Expected activity times and their standard deviations are computed in this manner for all the activities of the network and arranged in the tabular format as shown in Exhibit 14.

Exhibit 14: Computations of Expected Time and Standard Deviation

Activity	Predecessors	a	m	b	t_e	σ
A	None	1	3	5	3.0	.67
B	None	1	2	3	2.0	.33
C	A	1	1	7	2.0	1.00
D	B	7	9	17	10.0	1.67
E	B	2	2	2	2.0	0.00
F	E	2	5	8	5.0	.67
G	C,D,F	3	7	17	8.0	2.33
H	E	2	4	12	5.0	1.67

To answer the first question, we need to determine the network's critical path. A path is a sequence of connected activities. In Exhibit 2, 1-2-4-6 would be an example of a path. The critical path for a project is the path that takes the longest amount of time. The sum of the estimated times for all activities on the critical path is the total time required to complete the project. These activities are "critical" because any delay in their completion will cause a delay in the project.

The time to do all the activities on the critical path represents the minimum amount of time needed for the completion of the project. Thus, to speed up the project, the activities along this path must be shortened. Activities not on the critical path are not critical, since they will be worked on simultaneously with critical path activities and their completion could be delayed up to a point without delaying the project as a whole.

An easy way to find the critical path involves the following two steps:
1. Identify all possible paths of a project and calculate their completion times.
2. Pick the one with the longest amount of completion time, which is the critical path.

In the example, we have:

PATH	COMPLETION TIME
A-C-G	13 days (3 + 2 + 8)
B-D-G	20 days (2 + 10 + 8)
B-E-F-G	17 days (2 + 2 + 5 + 8)
B-E-H	9 days (2 + 2 + 5)

The critical path is B-D-G, which means it takes 20 days to complete the project.

The next important information we want to obtain is "what is the chance that the project will be completed within a contract time, say, 21 days?" To answer the question, we introduce the standard deviation of total project time around the expected time, which is determined as follows:

$$\text{Standard deviation (project)} = \sqrt{\text{the sum of the squares of the standard deviations of all critical path activities}}$$

Using the formula above, the standard deviation of completion time (the path B-D-G) for the project is as follows:

$$\sqrt{(.33)^2 + (1.67)^2 + (2.33)^2} = \sqrt{.1089 + 2.7889 + 5.4289}$$
$$= \sqrt{8.3267} = 2.885 \text{ days}$$

Using the standard deviation and table of areas under the normal distribution curve (Table 1 - Normal Distribution at the end of the chapter), the probability of completing the project within any given time period can be determined. Assume the expected delivery time is say, 21 days. The first step is to compute z, which is the number of standard deviations from the mean represented by our given time of 21 days. The formula for z is:

$$z = \frac{(\text{delivery time} - \text{expected delivery time})}{\text{standard deviation}}$$

Therefore,

$$z = \frac{(21 \text{ days} - 20 \text{ days})}{2.885 \text{ days}} = .35$$

The next step is to find the probability associated with the calculated value of z by referring to a table of areas under a normal curve.

From Table 1, we see the probability is .6368, which means there is close to a 64% chance that the project will be completed in less than 21 days.

To summarize what we have obtained,

1. The expected completion time of the project is 20 days.
2. There is a better than 60% chance of finishing before 21 days. *Note:* We can also obtain the chances of meeting any other deadline if we wish. All we need to do is change the delivery time and recalculate the z value.
3. Activities B-D-G are on the critical path; they must be watched more closely than the others, for if they fall behind, the whole project falls behind.
4. If extra effort is needed to finish the project on time or before the deadline, we have to borrow resources (such as money and labor) from any activity not on the critical path.

Summary of PERT Procedure

In analyzing any project using PERT, we perform the following steps:

Step 1: Develop a list of activities that make up the project, including immediate predecessors and draw a network corresponding to the activity list developed.

Step 2: Estimate the expected activity time and the variance for each activity.

Step 3: Using the expected activity time estimates, determine the earliest start time and the earliest finish time for each activity. The earliest finish time for the complete project corresponds to the earliest finish time for the last activity. This is the expected project completion time.

Step 4: Using the project completion time as the latest finishing time for the last activity, work backward through the network to compute the latest start and latest finish time for each activity.

Step 5: Compute the slack associated with each activity. The critical path activities are the activities with *zero* slack. The slack is the length of time an activity can be delayed without affecting the project completion date.

Step 6: Use the variability in the activity times to estimate the variability of the project completion date; then, using this estimate, compute the probability of meeting a specified completion date.

Steps to be Followed in Determining the Critical Path

When the network is large and complex, it is tedious to find the critical path by listing all the paths and picking the longest one. We need a more systematic and efficient approach, which is explained below.

Step 1: Find the earliest start (ES) and earliest finish (EF) times for the activities. This is done by assigning a start time (usually zero) for the initial job (s) and determining the earliest possible start time for each of the activities in the network. The rule is: since a job cannot be started until all preceding jobs have been finished, the earliest start time of an activity is the maximum of the earliest finish times of the immediate predecessors. The earliest finish time for an activity is its earliest start time plus the activity duration time (t). EF = ES + t.

Step 2: Compute the latest start (LS) and latest finish (LF) times for the activities. This is done by what is called a backward pass. We begin this time at the completion point. The latest finish time is the latest time at which an activity can be completed without extending the completion time of the network. The rule is: the latest finish time for an activity is the minimum of the latest start time of the immediately succeeding activities. The latest start time is the latest at which an activity can begin without extending the completion time of the project. It is the latest finish time minus the activity duration, LS = LF − t

Exhibit 15: Network Diagram

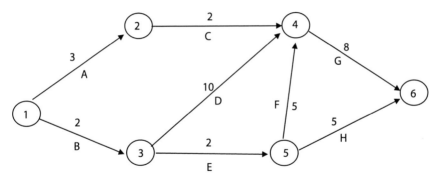

Step 3: Compute slack times for the activities. The critical path of the project is made up of those activities with zero slack. The slack is the length of the time we can delay an activity without interfering with the project completion. Any delay in completing activities on the critical path will result in a lengthening of the project duration.

Slack = ES - LS or EF - LF

In other words, we compare the earliest start time with the latest start time for any activity, i.e., we look at when it *can* be started and when it *must* be started to see how much free time, or slack, that activity has.

Exhibit 16 illustrates how the critical path is determined using this approach.

Exhibit 16: Determination of the Critical Path

ACTIVITY	ES	EF	LS	LF	SLACK =ES - LS OR EF - LF	ACTIVITY ON CRITICAL PATH
A	0	3	7	10	7	
B	0	2	0	2	0	Yes
C	3	5	10	12	7	
D	2	12	2	12	0	Yes
E	2	4	5	7	3	
F	4	9	7	12	3	
G	12	20	12	20	0	Yes
H	4	9	15	20	11	

The critical path with zero slacks (double lines) is shown in Exhibit 17.

Exhibit 17: Critical Path

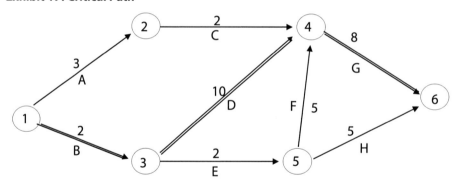

Note: It should be noted that PERT is a technique for project management and control. It is not an optimizing decision model since the decision to undertake a project is initially assumed. It will not evaluate an investment project according to its attractiveness or time specifications.

It is possible to reduce the completion time of one or more activities, which will require an extra expenditure of cost. The benefit from reducing the total completion time of a project by accelerated efforts on certain activities must be balanced against the extra cost of doing so. A related problem is to determine which activities must be accelerated to reduce the total project completion time. The *Critical Path Method (CPM)*, also known as *PERT/COST*, is widely used to deal with this subject.

The Critical Path Method (CPM) Model: PERT/COST

If the project duration (length of critical path) exceeds the allowable deadline, options include (1) changing the deadline or (2) "crashing" the project. Crashing means speeding up one or more activities along the critical path. This may involve shifting more resources (money) to those activities or perhaps outsourcing some of the work.

The critical path method (CPM) model, also known as PERT/COST, argues that most activities can be reduced in duration if extra resources (men, machines, money, and so on) are assigned to them. The cost for getting the job done may increase, but if other advantages outweigh this added cost, the job should be expedited or crashed. The CPM model attempts to solve (1) which jobs to crash and (2) by how much. The *normal time* is similar to the most likely time estimate in PERT. This could be viewed as the most efficient time to complete the project.

The *crash time* is the time required when extra resources are added to complete the project in the minimum possible time. Use of the crash time results in added costs for the project. A simplified view of the relationship between the normal and the crash times is seen in Exhibit 8. This represents a linear cost-time relationship. A nonlinear relationship is also possible, and may be more realistic. However, to illustrate the model, only the simplified linear relationship will be used. The slope of the cost-time line for any activity can be determined by the following:

$$\text{Slope} = \text{cost per day} \quad = \quad \frac{\text{Crash cost - Normal cost}}{\text{Normal time - Crash time}}$$

The slope of these lines actually measures the increase in cost per unit increase in time. Therefore, all such slopes are negative. The minus sign can be ignored and only absolute values considered, however.

To illustrate the CPM model, assume a simple project, as represented by the network diagram in Exhibit 8. The time, cost, and cost slope data for this project are shown in Exhibit 18.

Exhibit 18: Network Diagram for CPM Illustration

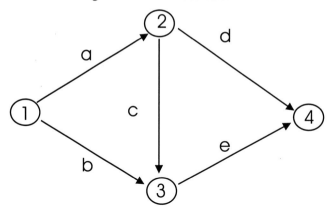

Normal Solution

From the foregoing information, the normal time solution can be developed. This solution is shown in Exhibit 19, with the appropriate normal time estimates indicated on the activity arrows. The critical path for this solution, as indicated by the heavy arrows, is a-c-e = 15 days. The total cost of the normal time solution is $3,900.

EXHIBIT 19: CPM Project Time and Cost Data

		TIME/DAYS		COST		
ACTIVITY	NORMAL	CRASH	NORMAL	CRASH	SLOPE
a	4	3	$ 400	$ 800	400
b	8	5	600	2,400	600
c	6	5	1,000	1,200	200
d	9	8	700	1,400	700
e	5	2	1,200	2,700	500
Total cost			$3,900	$8,500	

Crash Solution

The crash time solution can also be determined from the information in the same way. This solution is found in Exhibit 20. The critical path can be determined as a-d = 11 days, with a cost of $8,500.

Exhibit 20: Normal Time Solution CPM Network

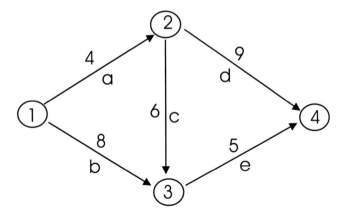

EXHIBIT 21: Crash Time Solution CPM Network

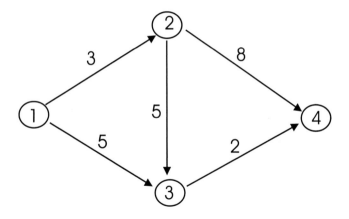

Determination of Minimum-COST Crash Solution

The crash solution set forth above indicated that this project can be completed in 11 days at a cost of $8,500. The next question for management to answer is whether the project can be completed in this same period of time for a lower cost.

The CPM (PERT/COST) model involves the following steps:

1. Find the *critical path*.
2. Look at all the slopes (crash costs per unit of time) for all activities on the critical path.
3. Pick the activity on the critical path with the lowest cost increase per unit of time. If there is a tie, pick one of the ties activities at random.

4. Use crash time on this activity, compute the expected total time, the total cost, and determine the new critical path.
5. Repeat the process until either the expected total time is equal to or less than the required time, there are no more possible time savings, *or* the total cost exceeds available funds.

Now we apply these steps to the example. First, we list all paths:

PATH	LENGTH	
a-c-e	15 ←	critical path
b-e	13	
a-d	13	

Next, we determine the critical path activities in the order of lowest crashing cost and the number of days that can be crashed.

ACTIVITY	SLOPE	AVAILABLE DAYS
c	200	1
a	400	1
e	500	3

Shorten c and a one day a piece at a cost of $600 ($200 +$400). The length of the path a-c-e becomes 13 days, which is the same as the length of paths b-e and a-d. Since all three paths are now critical further improvements will necessitate shorting one activity on each.

PATH	LENGTH
a-c-e	13 critical path
b-e	13 critical path
a-d	13 critical path

PATH	ACTIVITY	SLOPE
a-c-e	a	No reduction possible
	c	No reduction possible
	e	$500
b-e	b	$600
	e	No reduction possible
a-d	a	No reduction possible
	d	$700

The following three activities can be crashed:

ACTIVITY	SLOPE	AVAILABLE DAYS
e	500	3
b	600	3
d	700	1

Shortening activity e two days for $1,000 ($500 x 2) and d one day ($700) would lead to the critical paths a-c-e and a-d of 11 days for $6,200. While activity b can be crashed, their crashing does not reduce project duration. The minimum time of the project is 11 days at a cost of $6,200. At this point, no additional improvement is possible.

To summarize,

PROJECT TIME	CRASHING OPTIONS	LEAST COST OPTION	PROJECT COST	CRITICAL PATHS
15 days			$3,900	a-c-e
13	-1 at c & a ($200 + 400)	c & a	$4,500	a-c-e; b-d; a-d
11	-2 at e ($500 x 2) &	e & d	$6,200	a-c-e; a-d
	-1 at d ($700)			

Management Use of CPM

The CPM network has the primary goal of aiding management in the control of costs as well as of time. In these models, this goal is accomplished by providing management with a technique whereby the various time-cost trade-offs in a project can be evaluated. The process involves the determination of the lowest cost, longest completion time solution; and the shortest time, highest cost solution. From these two solutions, various alternatives can be established. For example, the lowest cost possible for the shortest completion time can be found. In addition, a variety of alternatives involving reduction in completion time and the added cost of each can be ascertained. Thus, the time and cost of completing the project under normal conditions, and the amount of time that can be saved by the expenditure of more money on various activities are determined. Management can then make a decision about the project after a consideration of all of the time-cost options. The lowest cost option, the shortest time option, and the interim alternatives with the appropriate cost and schedule data will be available.

Computer Software for Project Management

Most project management applications today use computers extensively. The management of projects is enhanced by tools such as *Gantt* charting, Fish-bone diagram, the *Program Evaluation and Review Technique (PERT)*, and *Critical Path Method (CPM)*. These tools are easily computerized and indeed there are dozens of commercial packages on the market. The user inputs activity time estimates and procedure information, program output slack for each activity, duration and variance for critical paths, and other useful project management information. Many project management software packages, such as Microsoft project, let planners enter defined activities, events, and times only once, and then present either a Gantt or a PERT chart-or both-on the computer's monitor. The project manager can then see how changing parameters will alter the charts and completion times. Some managers prefer using Gantt charts, some prefer PERT charts, and others use both, for the same projects. The preference depends on the personality of the manager and on presentation needs, rather than on the nature of the project.

The types of project management software are described below.

1. Project- and Resource-Tracking Software. With these applications, you enter each task and subtask of the project as well as each subproject, then define resources, such as employees and contractors, and assign them. Most of these tools let you define priorities and set the order in which subprojects or individual parts of the project must be done. Many good specialized project-tracking tools are available, but remember, spreadsheets and even text editors can do the job in a pinch. The quality of your project management depends more on your skill and attentiveness than on the tools you choose to use.

2. Time-Tracking Software. These applications let you track in detail the amount of time it takes to implement your project. Keeping abreast of this information over time will help you improve your estimating skills.

3. Bug-Tracking and Source-Code Version-Control Software. These applications are not just for software-development projects. You can use these products to control changes to documentation, keep on top of the versions of vendor software that are in your standard desktop image and track problems with every portion of your project.

Below is a list of project management software.

Project & Portfolio Management

Computer Associates International
www.ca.com

iPlan Project Management

Integrated Strategic Information Systems Pvt. Ltd.
www.iPlanEnterprise.com

Microsoft Project

Microsoft Corp.
www.microsoft.com

The Edge Solution w/Portfolio Edge & Project Office

Pacific Edge Software
www.pacificedge.com

PlanViewProject Management

PlanView
www.planview.com

Primavera

Oracle
www.oracle.com/primera

Deltek Cobra and Open Plan

Deltek

Om

www.deltek.com

@RISK for Project

Palisade Corporation
www.palisade.com

Serena Project Management

Serena Software
www.serena.com

Selecting a Project Management Software Package

Here are specific recommendations for project management software.

1. *Plan the project.* Plan a software acquisition project to ensure you have overall agreement on the objectives, deliverables, scope, time frame, approach, etc., for choosing the software. This should include the background on what type of tool you will be considering, why it is needed, where it will fit in your technology architecture, etc. You should also build the work plan that you will use to manage the project. This planning step takes place just as it would for any projects that you manage.

2. *Gather and rank business requirements.* It's hard to select a tool or package if you are not sure what your requirements are. Again, this work is similar to the analysis you would do for any project. Ask questions such as the following:

   ▶ What will people be using the package for?
   ▶ What problem will the package solve?
   ▶ What features and functions are required?

Many times, you will not be able to determine all the requirements by just asking the customers. You can look for other potential requirements by reviewing prior research from industry analysts, reading magazines and periodicals, and searching the Web. These searches can be used to generate potential requirements that can be validated by your customers. Each requirement should be weighted on a numeric scale, or rank ordered from high to low for example, to reflect the relative importance of some requirements over others. (Other weighting scales can be utilized as well). This total list of requirements and weightings need to be reviewed and approved by your sponsor and major customers and stakeholders.

3. *Create package long list.* At this point, look for any and all packages that might meet your needs. This can be accomplished by searching the Web, looking at trade magazines, talking to other companies, etc. The purpose of the step is to gather a comprehensive, but not exhaustive, list of vendors and packages that you want to consider further. If you think you already know the particular packages you are interested in, this step can be skipped, moving you directly to the short list. But this step helps ensure that there is not an obvious candidate that you are overlooking.

4. *Create package short list.* Perform an initial, high-level evaluation of the long list, looking for obvious reasons to eliminate some of the alternatives. For example, certain products may not fit within your technology architecture, some may be too new, or some may be obviously too expensive. In some cases, there may be a feature that you absolutely need that is not available. The purpose of this step is to create a short list of potential packages that look

like they will have a reasonable chance to meet your needs. If the long list is not too large, you could send a Request for Proposal (RFP) to each candidate for feedback. You could also ask for product brochures and other literature. But, you must narrow down the packages to a small enough number that you can compare and contrast the remaining solutions reasonable during your final selection process.

5. *Evaluate package short list.* This step can be the most difficult part of package selection. You must map the package features and functions against your requirements and weighting factors to determine which package most closely meets your needs. If you did not send out an RFP to the long list, you might want to send one out now to the short list. You can also interview the vendors, set up product demonstrations, and make vendor site visits. Usually, some type of numerical calculation is made based on how well the package meets each requirement, multiplied by the weighting factor. The package with the highest score across all requirements should be the one that best meets your needs. When you have completed this step, you should have a first and second choice for the package that best meets your needs.

6. *Make final selection and negotiate contract.* In many organizations, the project team makes the final recommendation and then turns the process over to a formal purchasing or procurement organization. They are responsible for contract negotiation and legal details.

You should have an understanding now of the basic process that can be used to make a package or vendor selection. Of course, if the software is complex and expensive, these high-level processes might be broken down into 100 distinct activities. In fact, for large, strategic purchases, such as with the Department of Defense, the selection process could take months or years. On the other hand, for simpler, commonly used packages, the process might be streamlined and completed in a matter of days or weeks.

Still, you must understand your requirements first and then go through a process of finding and subsequently narrowing down the field of potential packages and vendors until you can make an intelligent decision on which one to purchase. Here are some of the factors you should consider, examine, and compare before selecting the "right" software for you.

Cost vs. Functionality. The costs and capabilities of project management software vary considerably. Systems can cost anywhere from a few hundred dollars to tens of thousands of dollars. Consider how much power you need with respect to the size of project the software can handle and the features you're likely to need or benefit from. Make sure you keep an eye to the future: consider functionality not only in terms of what you need now, but for the long term as well.

Capability vs. Ease of Use: There's a general relationship between the capability of project management software and its ease of use. Consider this example. A company wanted to purchase project management software and knew that they did not require a great deal of computing power. However, the decision-makers felt that they wanted maximum horsepower in their software, "just in case." Unfortunately, proper use of the software required sending people off to a month-long, intensive training program and to periodic refresher courses, thereafter. The company had difficulty breaking people free to take the training. After two years of hacking their way through the use of the tool, they abandoned it and bought something simpler.

Compatibility with other Systems: Consider how your project management software will have to interface with other communication, accounting, or reporting systems already in use in your company.

Documentation, Startup Support and Ongoing Technical Support: How much support can you expect from the manufacturer and/or the company selling the software? Consider important issues, such as the documentation you'll receive, the setup and startup support you can expect, and the long-term technical support you'll get.

Consider using several sources of input, including the experiences of others and rating guides, before making your final selection of project management software.

A Caveat

The tremendous power of project management software can lull you into a false sense of security. Although the tool can save you a significant amount of time, there are many things that it cannot do. For these, you'll have to rely upon your knowledge of project management rather than the tool. Here are some things that the tool cannot do:

▶ *Make decisions*: You'll still have to determine the course of the project through the day-to-day decisions you make
▶ *Gather data*: You must still determine how much data you need and what forms are most useful to manage your project.
▶ *Find errors:* If you input bad data, you will get bad data out
▶ *Solve your most critical problems*: Some of the biggest problems you encounter will relate to people. Obviously, project management software does not address this issue at all.

Table 1: Normal Distribution Table

Areas under the normal curve

Z	0	1	2	3	4	5	6	7	8	9
0.0	0.5000	0.5040	0.5080	0.5120	0.5160	0.5199	0.5239	0.5279	0.5319	0.5359
0.1	0.5398	0.5438	0.5478	0.5517	0.5557	0.5596	0.5636	0.5675	0.5714	0.5753
0.2	0.5793	0.5832	0.5871	0.5910	0.5948	0.5987	0.6026	0.6064	0.6103	0.6141
0.3	0.6179	0.6217	0.6255	0.6293	0.6331	0.6368	0.6406	0.6443	0.6480	0.6517
0.4	0.6554	0.6591	0.6628	0.6664	0.6700	0.6736	0.6772	0.6808	0.6844	0.6879
0.5	0.6915	0.6950	0.6985	0.7019	0.7054	0.7088	0.7123	0.7157	0.7190	0.7224
0.6	0.7257	0.7291	0.7324	0.7357	0.7389	0.7422	0.7454	0.7486	0.7517	0.7549
0.7	0.7580	0.7611	0.7642	0.7673	0.7703	0.7734	0.7764	0.7794	0.7823	0.7852
0.8	0.7881	0.7910	0.7939	0.7967	0.7995	0.8023	0.8051	0.8078	0.8106	0.8133
0.9	0.8159	0.8186	0.8212	0.8238	0.8264	0.8289	0.8315	0.8340	0.8365	0.8389
1.0	0.8413	0.8438	0.8461	0.8485	0.8508	0.8531	0.8554	0.8577	0.8599	0.8621
1.1	0.8643	0.8665	0.8686	0.8708	0.8729	0.8749	0.8770	0.8790	0.8810	0.8830
1.2	0.8849	0.8869	0.8888	0.8907	0.8925	0.8944	0.8962	0.8980	0.8997	0.9015
1.3	0.9032	0.9049	0.9066	0.9082	0.9099	0.9115	0.9131	0.9147	0.9162	0.9177
1.4	0.9192	0.9207	0.9222	0.9236	0.9251	0.9265	0.9278	0.9292	0.9306	0.9319
1.5	0.9332	0.9345	0.9357	0.9370	0.9382	0.9394	0.9406	0.9418	0.9430	0.9441
1.6	0.9452	0.9463	0.9474	0.9484	0.9495	0.9505	0.9515	0.9525	0.9535	0.9545
1.7	0.9554	0.9564	0.9573	0.9582	0.9591	0.9599	0.9608	0.9616	0.9625	0.9633
1.8	0.9641	0.9648	0.9656	0.9664	0.9671	0.9678	0.9686	0.9693	0.9700	0.9706
1.9	0.9713	0.9719	0.9726	0.9732	0.9738	0.9744	0.9750	0.9756	0.9762	0.9767
2.0	0.9772	0.9778	0.9783	0.9788	0.9793	0.9798	0.9803	0.9808	0.9812	0.9817
2.1	0.9821	0.9826	0.9830	0.9834	0.9838	0.9842	0.9846	0.9850	0.9854	0.9857
2.2	0.9861	0.9864	0.9868	0.9871	0.9874	0.9878	0.9881	0.9884	0.9887	0.9890
2.3	0.9893	0.9896	0.9898	0.9901	0.9904	0.9906	0.9909	0.9911	0.9913	0.9916
2.4	0.9918	0.9920	0.9922	0.9925	0.9927	0.9929	0.9931	0.9932	0.9934	0.9936
2.5	0.9938	0.9940	0.9941	0.9943	0.9945	0.9946	0.9948	0.9949	0.9951	0.9952
2.6	0.9953	0.9955	0.9956	0.9957	0.9959	0.9960	0.9961	0.9962	0.9963	0.9964
2.7	0.9965	0.9966	0.9967	0.9968	0.9969	0.9970	0.9971	0.9972	0.9973	0.9974
2.8	0.9974	0.9975	0.9976	0.9977	0.9977	0.9978	0.9979	0.9979	0.9980	0.9981
2.9	0.9981	0.9982	0.9982	0.9983	0.9984	0.9984	0.9985	0.9985	0.9986	0.9986
3.0	0.9987	0.9990	0.9993	0.9995	0.9997	0.9998	0.9998	0.9999	0.9999	1.0000

CHAPTER 6

Project Control and Evaluation

Every step taken up to now has been for one purpose – to achieve control of the project. This is what is expected of a project manager – that organization resources be managed in such a way that critical results are achieved.

Characteristics of a Project Control System

The control system must focus on project objectives, with the aim of ensuring that the project mission is achieved. To do that, the control system should be designed with these questions in mind:

▶ What is important to the organization?
▶ What are we attempting to do?
▶ Which aspects of the work are most important to track and control?
▶ What are the critical points in the process at which controls should be placed?

Control should be exercised over what is important. On the other hand, what is controlled also tends to become important. Thus, if budgets and schedules are emphasized to the exclusion of quality, only those will be controlled. The project may well come in on time and within budget, but at the expense of quality. Project managers must monitor performance carefully to ensure that quality does not suffer.

Project Review Meetings

There are two aspects to project control. One can be called maintenance and the other aims at improvement of performance. The maintenance review just tries to keep the project on track. The improvement review tries to help project teams improve performance. Three kinds of reviews are routinely conducted to achieve these purposes. They are:

▶ Status reviews
▶ Process or lessons-learned reviews
▶ Design reviews

Everyone should do status and process reviews. Design reviews, of course, are appropriate only if you are designing hardware, software, or some sort of campaign, such as a marketing campaign.

A status review is aimed at maintenance. It asks where the project stands. Process means the way something is done, and you can be sure that process always affects task performance. That is, *how* something is done affects the outcome. For that reason, process improvement is the work of every manager. How this is done is covered in the next section.

Project Evaluation

As the dictionary definition says, to evaluate a project is to attempt to determine whether the overall status of the work is acceptable, in terms of intended value to the client once the job is finished. Project evaluation appraises the progress and performance of a job compared to what was originally planned. That evaluation provides the basis for management decisions on how to proceed with the project. The evaluation must be credible in the eyes of everyone affected, or decisions based on it will not be considered valid. The primary tool for project evaluation is the *project process review*, which is usually conducted at major milestones throughout the life of the project.

Purposes of Project Evaluation

Sports teams that practice without reviewing performance may get really good at playing very badly. That is why they review game films – to see where they need to improve. In other words, the purpose of a review is to learn lessons that can help the team to avoid doing things that cause undesired outcomes and to continue those that help. The review should be called a *lessons-learned* or *process review*.

You might deliberately avoid the word *audit*, because nobody likes to be audited. Historically, an audit has been designed to catch people doing things they shouldn't have done so that they could be penalized in some way. If you go around auditing people, you can be sure they will hide from you anything they don't want you to know, and it is those very things that could help the company learn and grow.

There are two kinds of organizations in this world today – those that are getting better and those that are dying. An organization that stands still is dying. It just doesn't know it yet. The competition is not sitting by idly. It is doing new things, some of which may be better than yours. If you aren't constantly improving, you will be passed by, and soon you won't have a market.

The same is true of every part of an organization. You can't sub-optimize, improving just manufacturing. You have to improve every department, and that includes how you run projects.

In fact, good project management can give you a real competitive advantage, especially in product development. If you are sloppy in managing your projects, you don't have good control of development costs. That means that you have to either sell a lot of product or change large margins to cover your development costs so that the project is worth doing in the first place. If you can't sell a lot of widgets, then you have to charge the large margin. If you competitor, on the other hand, has good cost control, it can charge smaller margins and still be sure that it recovers its investment and makes money. Thus, it has a competitive advantage over you because of its better *control* of project work.

Additionally, in order to learn, people require feedback, like that gained by a team from reviewing game films. The last phase of a project should be a final process review, conducted so that the management of projects can be improved. However, such a process review should not be conducted only at the end of the project. Rather, process reviews should be done at major milestones in the project or every three months, whichever comes first, so that learning can take place as the job progresses. Furthermore, if a project is getting into serious trouble, the process review should reveal the difficulty so that a decision can be made to continue or terminated the work.

Following are some of the general reasons for conducting periodic project process reviews. Successful process reviews should help to:

▷ Improve project performance together with the management of the project.

▷ Ensure that quality of project work does not take a back seat to schedule and cost concerns.

▷ Reveal developing problems early so that action can be taken to deal with them.

▷ Identify areas where other projects (current or future) should be managed differently.

▷ Keep client(s) informed of project status. This can also help ensure that the completed project will meet the needs of the client.

▷ Reaffirm the organization's commitment to the project for the benefit of project team members.

Conducting the Project Process Review

Ideally, a project process review should be conducted by an independent examiner, who can remain objective in the assessment of information. However, the process review must be conducted in a spirit of learning, rather than in a climate of blame and punishment. If people are afraid that they will be "strung up" for problems, then they will hide those problems and likely many other things as well .

Even so, openness is hard to achieve. In many organizations, the climate has been punitive for so long that people are reluctant to reveal any less-than-perfect aspects of project performance.

Two questions should be asked in the review. The first is, "What have we done well so far?," and the second is, "What do we want to improve (or do better) in the future?" Notice that the question is not, "What have we done badly?" That question serves only to make everyone defensive, because they assume that you will punish them for things done wrong. Furthermore, there is always the possibility that nothing has been done wrong, but there is always room to improve.

Finally, the results of the review should be published. Otherwise, the only people in the organization who can take advantage of it are the members of the team just reviewed. If other teams know what was learned, then they can benefit from that information. In the next section, we look at what the report should contain.

The Process Review Report

A company may decide to conduct process reviews in varying degrees of thoroughness, from totally comprehensive, to partial, to less formal and cursory. A formal, comprehensive process review should be followed by a report. The report should contain as a minimum the following:

> ▶ *Current project status.* The best way to do this is to use earned value analysis, as presented in the following chapter. However, when earned value analysis is not used, status should still be reported with as great accuracy as possible.
> ▶ *Future status.* This is a forecast of what is expected to happen in the project. Are significant deviations expected in schedule, cost, performance, or scope? If so, the report should specify the nature of the changes.
> ▶ *Status of critical tasks.* The report should describe the status of critical tasks, particularly those on the critical path. Tasks that have high levels of technical risk should be given special attention, as should those being performed by outside vendors or subcontractors, over which the project manager may have limited control.
> ▶ *Risk assessment.* The report should mention any identified risks that could lead to monetary loss, project failure, or other liabilities.
> ▶ *Information relevant to other projects.* The report should describe what has been learned from this process review that can/should be applied to other projects, whether in progress or about to start.

▶ *Limitations of the process review.* The report should mention any factors that may limit the validity of the process review. Are any assumptions suspect? Are any data missing or perhaps contaminated? Was anyone uncooperative in providing information for the process review?

As a general comment, the simpler and more straightforward a project process review report, the better. The information should be organized so that planned versus actual results can be easily compared. Significant deviations should be highlighted and explained.

Critical Success Factors

A study was conducted to test the importance of certain factors that were believed to be critical to project success. Although the researchers specifically studied information systems projects, they pointed out that the factors presented were general enough to apply to almost any type of project. Seventy-eight survey questionnaires were obtained from fifty different firms. The results showed that the top ten major factors were:

1. Clearly defined goals and project mission
2. Top management support
3. A competent project manager
4. A competent project team
5. Sufficient resources
6. Client/customer involvement and consultation
7. Good communications
8. Responsiveness to clients
9. Proper monitoring and feedback
10. Appropriate technology

Source: J. Jiang, G. Klein, and J. Blloun, "Ranking of System Implementation Success Facors," *Project Management Journal*, December 1996.

CHAPTER 7

Project Control Using Earned Value Analysis

Why Do Some Projects Overrun the Budget?

Many project management gurus agree that poor cost control is what often puts a project in danger of exceeding the budget. They offer the following insights into why these pitfalls occur:

1. Many cost overruns stem from poor cost estimates.
2. In many companies there is no standardization or common set of rules for developing cost estimates and cost-control techniques, and neither is given very much importance.
3. Many people believe that because of the huge number of variables in a project, overruns are simply unavoidable—a devastating way of thinking, especially since it is not true.
4. Project plans and controls often don't take into account probabilistic measures.

In addition to establishing a baseline schedule for a project, it's also necessary to develop a baseline budget. Project costs are estimated when a proposal is prepared for the project. Once a decision is made to go forward with the proposed project, it's necessary to prepare a budget, or plan, for how and when funds will be spent over the duration of the project. Once the project starts, it's important to monitor actual costs and work performance to ensure that everything is within budget. At regular intervals during the project, the following cost—related parameters should be monitored:

▶ Cumulative actual amount spent since the start of the project

▶ Cumulative earned value of the work performed since the start of the project

▶ Cumulative budgeted amount planned to be spent, based on the project schedule, from the start of the project

Comparisons must be made among these three parameters to evaluate whether the project is being accomplished within budget and whether the value of the work performed is in line with the actual amount expended.

If at any time during the project it is determined that the project is overrunning the budget or the value of the work performed isn't keeping up with the actual amount expended, corrective action must be taken. Once project costs get out of control, it will be very difficult to complete the project within budget. As you will see in this chapter, the key to effective cost control is to analyze cost performance on a timely and regular basis. Early identification of cost variances allows corrective action to be taken before the situation gets worse. In this chapter, you will learn how to regularly forecast, based on the actual amount spent and the value of the work performed, whether the entire project will be completed within budget. You will become familiar with

▶ Items to be considered when estimating project cost

▶ Preparation of a baseline budget, or plan, for how and when funds will be spent over the duration of the project

▶ Cumulating actual costs

▶ Determining the earned value of the work performed

▶ Analyzing cost performance

▶ Forecasting project cost at completion

▶ Controlling project costs

▶ Managing cash flow

Project Budgeting and Cost Estimates

Cost planning starts with the proposal for the project. It is during the development of the proposal by the contractor or project team that project costs are estimated. In some cases, the proposal will indicate only the total bottom-line cost for the proposed project. In other cases, the customer may request a detailed breakdown of various costs. The cost section of a proposal may consist of tabulations of the contractor's estimated costs for such elements as the following:

1. *Labor.* This portion gives the estimated costs for the various classifications of people who are expected to work on the project, such as painters, designers, and computer programmers. It might include the estimated hours and hourly rate for each person or classification.

2. *Materials.* This portion gives the cost of materials the contractor or project team needs to purchase for the project, such as paint, lumber, wallpaper, shrubbery, carpeting, paper, art supplies, food, computers, or software packages.

3. *Subcontractors and consultants.* When contractors or project teams do not have the expertise or resources to do certain project tasks, they may hire subcontractors or consultants to perform those tasks. Examples of such tasks include designing a brochure, developing a training manual, developing software, and catering a reception.

4. *Equipment and facilities rental.* Sometimes the contractor may need special equipment, tools, or facilities solely for the project. The equipment may be too expensive to purchase if it's going to be used on only one or a few projects. In such cases, the contractor may decide to rent the equipment for as long as it is needed on the project.

5. *Travel.* If travel (other than local travel) is required during the project, the costs for travel (such as airfare), hotel rooms, and meals need to be included.

In addition to the above items, the contractor or project team may include an amount for contingencies, to cover unexpected situations that may come up during the project. For example, items may have been overlooked when the project cost estimates were prepared, tasks may have to be redone because they did not work the first time, or the costs of labor (wages, salaries) or materials may escalate during a multiyear project.

It is good practice to have the person who will be responsible for the costs associated with the work make the cost estimates. This generates a commitment from the responsible person and prevents any bias that might result from having one person make all the cost estimates for the entire project. In large projects involving several hundred people, it is not practical to have every person provide cost estimates. In such cases, each organization or subcontractor involved may designate an experienced individual to make the cost estimates for which that organization or subcontractor will be responsible. If a contractor or organization has performed similar projects in the past and has kept records of the actual costs for various items, these historical data can be used as guides in estimating costs on the current project.

Cost estimates should be aggressive yet realistic. They should not be so heavily "padded" that they include contingency funds for every conceivable thing that might come up or go wrong. If cost estimates are overly conservative, the total estimated cost for the project is likely to be more than the customer is willing to pay—and higher than that of competing contractors. On the other hand, if cost estimates are overly optimistic and some unexpected expenditures need to be made, the contractor is likely to either lose money (on a fixed—price contract) or have to suffer the embarrassment of going back to the customer to request additional funds to cover cost overruns.

How do You Prepare Project Budgeting?

There are several alternatives for assessing budgets over time. Fixed costs may be expensed at the start of the activity (for example, equipment purchases) or at the end of the activity (e.g., paying a consultant) Variable costs may be expensed based on the project schedule or on the employee's calendar (for example, payroll).

Example 1

Exhibit 22 shows that a project has the budgeted costs associated with five activities. Assume that variable costs are incurred in proportion to the activity duration; thus, for instance, the cost for task B is spread out over the 2 weeks the task is scheduled. The resulting cost schedule is referred to as the *Budgeted Cost of Work Scheduled (BCWS)* and is calculated by adding all the costs on each week of the project as shown in the last two lines of the table.

Exhibit 22: Project Budgeting Example

TASK	PREDECESSOR	DURATION	COST	BY WEEK				
A	--	1	$1,500	$1,500				
B	A	2	$3,510		$1,755	$1,755		
C	A	2	$5,000		$2,500	$2,500		
D	B	2	$2,000				$1,000	$1,000
E	B	2	$3,000				$1,500	$1,500
Total project budget			$15,010	$1,500	$4,255	$4,255	$2,500	$2,500
Cumulative project budget = budgeted cost of work scheduled (BCWS)				$1,500	$5,755	$10,010	$12,510	$15,010

By accurately tracking actual costs versus budgeted costs, the project manager can obtain a better idea of the amount of managerial flexibility available. Thus, BCWS information is very useful for the project manager for controlling the project. For example, if by week 4 the project costs have exceeded $12,510, then the project manager might wish to control future expenses more carefully, renegotiate the contract with the customer, and/or try to get more funds in order to complete the project. Similarly, if the project incurs less cost by week 4, this might indicate that the project is behind schedule and the pace of work needs to pick up. But how can a manager tell whether a cost overrun is due to greater expense than expected or to the work being completed faster than expected? Earned value analysis resolves this dilemma.

The Whys of the Concept of Earned Value

Performing a separate analysis of schedule and cost does not provide an entirely accurate or comprehensive picture of overall project status. Evaluating how much work you're getting done without considering how much you've paid to get that work done will give you a distorted picture of your cost position. Similarly, using your rate of expenditure as a measure of project status will lead to a distorted picture of your schedule position. For example, you're under budget by about 10%. Good news, right? What if you are told that the project is nearly completed? Good news becomes unbelievably great news: you're nearly done and you've spent only about 75% of the money. Now imagine that the team has just barely gotten started; not much of anything has been done. This would be a disastrous situation.

The *earned value concept* integrates schedule and cost. There are a number of formulas associated with earned value techniques. At the core of the earned value technique are these three basic components of measurement:

- Budgeted Cost of Work Scheduled (BCWS)
- Budgeted Cost of Work Performed (BCWP)
- Actual Cost of Work Performed (ACWP)

Budgeted Cost of Work Scheduled (BCWS) is a measure of *what* you *expect* to *accomplish*. Specifically, it uses the original cost estimates for activities to chart the cost (or value) of the work that you plan to get done over time. It's equivalent to the conventional concept of the "planned budget."

Budgeted Cost of Work Performed (BCWP) is a measure of *the value of what you've actually accomplished.* It charts the cost (or value) of the work you've gotten done at any point in time. Again, the original activity-based cost estimates are used to perform these calculations. This is what "earned value" actually is.

Actual Cost of Work Performed (ACWP) refers to *what* you *paid for what you've accomplished.* This would be your actual cost expenditure at any point in time.

Conceptually, your schedule position is a comparison of BCWP and BCWS. In other words (using the terminology above), it compares *what you expected* to *accomplish* and *what you've actually accomplished,* in terms of originally estimated dollar amounts.

Your cost position can be evaluated by comparing BCWP and ACWP, in other words, *what* you *thought you'd have* to *pay* and *what you've actually paid—for a given amount of accomplishment*

Earned value analysis is a project performance measurement technique that integrates scope, time, and cost data. It is an approach for monitoring project costs and expenses. It involves specifying, on a periodic basis, how far each activity has progressed (**% complete**) and deriving the value of work completed from this information. Value is "earned" as activities are completed. The cumulative value of work completed on any week is then compared to actual costs incurred in completing that work and the amount of work budgeted for completion. Earned value is a uniform unit of measure and thus provides a consistent method for analyzing project progress and performance.

Establishing an earned value analysis system involves the following steps:

1. Establishing the work breakdown structure (WBS) to divide the project into manageable portions.
2. Identifying the activities to be scheduled.
3. Allocating the costs to be expended on each activity.
4. Scheduling the activities over time and assess percent completion.
5. Tabulating, plotting, and analyzing the data to confirm that the plan is acceptable.

Example 2

In Example 1, suppose that on week 4, a manager assesses the actual costs and % complete for each activity as shown in Exhibit 2.

Exhibit 23: Earned Value Data

Task	Pre-decessor	Duration	Budgeted Cost	Actual Cost	% Complete	Earned Value = Budgeted Cost x % Complete	By week Allocated Cost				
A	–	1	$1,500	$1,600	100	$1,500	$1,500				
B	A	2	$3,510	$3,700	100	$3,510		$1,755	$1,755		
C	A	2	$5,000	$4,600	80	$4,000		$2,500	$2,500		
D	B	2	$2,000	$1,000	60	$1,200				$1,000	$1,000
E	B	2	$3,000	$500	10	$300				$1,500	$1,500
Total costs			$15,010	$11,400		$10,510	$1,500	$4,255	$4,255	$2,500	$2,500
Cumulative costs by period							$1,500	$5,755	$10,010	$12,510	$15,010

The earned value is calculated by multiplying the budgeted cost of the activity by the % complete and then adding the result over all activities (see Exhibit 3). For instance, on week 4, the status of the project is:

▶ Budgeted Cost of Work Scheduled (BCWS) = $12,510

▶ Actual Cost of Work Performed (ACWP) = $11,400
▶ Budgeted Cost of Work Performed (BCWP) = $10,510 (earned value by week 4)

Exhibit 24: Cumulative Budgeted, Actual, and Earned Value: BCWS, ACWP, and CCWP

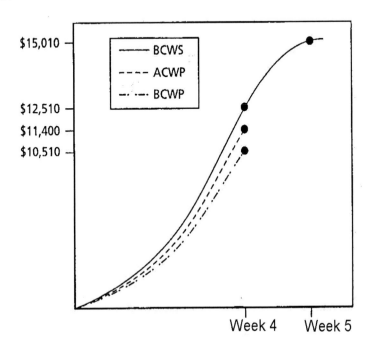

The distinction between the BCWS and the BCWP is that the former represents the budget of the activities that were planned to be completed, and the latter represents the budget of the activities that actually were completed. BCWP is often referred to as *earned value*. In this case, the good news is that actual costs are less then planned costs (see Exhibit 1); however, the bad news is that work accomplished on the project is less than anticipated. For example, activity C should have been finished but is only 80 percent complete.

Forecasting Project Parameters Using Earned Value Methodology

Earned value methodology can be used for forecasting the estimated completion time and costs of a project given the current status of the project. To distinguish between cost slippage and schedule slippage on the project, we define

Schedule Variance (SV)

Scheduled variance (SV) is the budgeted cost of work performed minus the budgeted cost of work scheduled = BCWP – BCWS. Schedule variance shows the difference between the scheduled completion of an activity and the actual completion of that activity. A negative schedule variance means it took longer than planned to perform the work, and a positive schedule variance means it took less time than planned to perform the work.

Cost Variance (CV)

Cost variance (CV) is the budgeted cost of work performed minus the actual cost of work performed = BCWP – ACWP. In other words, cost variance shows the difference between the estimated cost of an activity and the actual cost of that activity. If cost variance is a negative number, it means performing the work cost more than planned. If cost variance is a positive number, it means performing the work cost less than planned.

Example 3

In our example project at week 4, we compute SV = $10,510 - $12,510 = ($2,000) and CV = $10,510 - $11,400 = ($890).The value of SV indicates that the project is severely behind schedule, and CV indicates that we are also overspending on the project because work with a value of $10,510 was done by actually spending $11,400.

We can forecast that, given the pace of work, the project is going to take longer than 5 weeks, and with the unfavorable cost variance, it is going to cost more than $15,010.

These forecasts can be made by calculating the following performance indices.

The Schedule Performance Index (SPI)

The schedule performance index (SP1) is the ratio of work performed to work scheduled (BCWP/BCWS) and can be used to estimate the projected time to complete the project.. A schedule performance index of one or 100 percent means the project is on schedule. If the schedule performance index is greater than one or 100 percent, then the project is ahead of schedule. If the schedule performance index is less than one or 100 percent, the project is behind schedule.

The Cost Performance Index (CPI)

The cost performance index (CPI) is the ratio of work performed to actual costs (BCWP/ACWP) and can be used to estimate the projected cost of completing the project. If the cost performance index is equal to one, then the budged and actual costs are equal, or the costs are exactly as planned. If the cost performance index is less than one or less than 100 percent, the project is over budget. If the cost performance index is greater than one or more than 100 percent, the project is under budget.

Note: Inn general, negative numbers for cost and schedule variance indicate problems in those areas. The project is costing more than planned or taking longer than planned. Likewise, CPI and SPI less than 100 percent also indicate problems. Earned value calculations for all project activities (or summary level activities) are required to estimate the earned value for the entire project. Some activities may be over budget or behind schedule, but others may be under budget and ahead of schedule. By adding all of the earned values for all project activities, you can determine how the project as a whole is performing.

The Estimate at Completion (EAC)

The Estimate at Completion (EAC) is an estimate of what it will cost to complete the project based on performance to date. It indicates where the project cost is heading. One simple way to calculate this is

$$EAC = (BAG - BCWP)/CPI + ACWP$$

where BAG = budget at completion, the initial budget for the project.

This formula determines the unfinished or unearned work (BAG - BCWP) and divides it by the CPI. To that is added the sunk cost, or the cost of the completed work (ACWP). From this we can see that poor cost performance, a CPI less than 1, would result in an EAC that is greater than the BAG.

Example 4

For our example project, these calculations are

$$SPI = \$10,510/\$12,510 = 0.84$$

$$CPI = \$10,510/\$11,400 = 0.92$$

$$EAC = (\$15,010 - \$10,510)/0.92 + \$11,400 = \$4,891.07 + \$11,400 = \$16,291.07$$

A similar forecast can be made for the project duration using the SPI; if work progresses at the current pace (84% schedule efficiency), then the time to complete the project would be

Estimated time to complete the project = original project duration/SPI = 5/0.84 = 5.95 weeks

Estimated cost at completion = planned cost/CPI = $10,510/0.92 =$12,424

Cost Control

The key to effective cost control is to analyze cost performance on a regular and timely basis. It's crucial that cost variances and inefficiencies be identified early so that corrective action can be taken before the situation gets worse. Once project costs get out of control, it may be very difficult to complete the project within budget.

Cost control involves the following:

1. Analyzing cost performance to determine which work packages may require corrective action
2. Deciding what specific corrective action should be taken
3. Revising the project plan—including time and cost estimates—to incorporate the planned corrective action

The cost performance analysis should include identifying those work packages that have a negative cost variance or a cost performance index of less than 1.0. Also, those work packages for which the CV or GPI has deteriorated since the prior reporting period should be identified. A concentrated effort must be applied to the work packages with negative variances, to reduce cost or improve the efficiency of the work performed. The amount of CV should determine the priority for applying these concentrated efforts; that is, the work package with the largest negative CV should be given top priority.

When evaluating work packages that have a negative cost variance, you should focus on taking corrective actions to reduce the costs of two types of activities:

1. *Activities that will be performed in the near term.* Don't plan to reduce the costs of activities that are scheduled sometime in the distant future. You'll get more timely feedback on the effects of corrective actions if they are done in the near term. If you put off corrective actions until some point in the distant future, the negative cost variance may deteriorate even further before the corrective actions are ever implemented. As the project progresses, less and less time remains in which corrective actions can be taken.
2. *Activities that have a large cost estimate.* Taking corrective measures that reduce the cost of a $20,000 activity by 10 percent will have a larger impact than totally eliminating a $300 activity. Usually, the larger the estimated cost for an activity, the greater the opportunity for a large cost reduction.

There are various ways to reduce the costs of activities. One way is to substitute less expensive materials that meet the required specifications. Maybe another supplier can be found who can supply the same material but at a lower cost. Another approach is to assign a person with greater expertise or more experience to perform or help with the activity so as to get it done more efficiently.

Reducing the scope or requirements for the work package or specific activities is another way to reduce costs. For example, a contractor might decide to put only one coat of paint on a room rather than two coats, as originally planned. Increasing productivity through improved methods or technology is yet another approach to reducing costs. For example, by renting automatic paint spraying equipment, a contractor may substantially reduce the cost and time of painting a room below what it would be for painters working with rollers and brushes.

In many cases, there will be a trade-off—reducing cost variances will involve a reduction in project scope or a delay in the project schedule. If the negative cost variance is very large, a substantial reduction in the work scope or quality may be required to get the project back within budget. The scope, budget, schedule, or quality of the overall project could be in jeopardy. In some cases, the customer and contractor or project team may have to acknowledge that one or more of these elements cannot be achieved. This could result in the customer's providing additional funds to cover the forecasted overrun, or it could result in a contract dispute over who caused the cost overrun and who should pay for it—the customer or the contractor.

The key to effective cost control is aggressively addressing negative cost variances and cost inefficiencies as soon as they are identified, rather than hoping that things will get better as the project goes on. Cost problems that are addressed early will have less impact on scope and schedule. Once costs get out of control, getting back within budget is likely to require reducing the project scope or extending the project schedule.

Even when projects have only positive cost variances, it's important not to let the cost variances deteriorate. If a project's cost performance is positive, a concentrated effort should be made to keep it that way. Once a project gets in trouble with cost performance, it becomes difficult to get back on track.

Managing Cash Flow

It is important to manage the cash flow on a project. Managing cash flow involves making sure that sufficient payments are received from the customer in time so that you have enough money to cover the costs of performing the project—employee payroll, charges for materials, invoices from subcontractors, and travel expenses, for example.

The key to managing cash flow is to ensure that cash comes in faster than it goes out. If sufficient cash isn't available to meet expenses, money must be borrowed. Borrowing increases project cost because any money borrowed must be paid back to the lender, along with a charge for borrowing the money—the interest.

The flow of cash coming in from the customer can be controlled by the terms of payment in the contract. From the contractor's point of view, it's desirable to receive payments from the customer early in the project rather than later. The contractor might try to negotiate payment terms that require the customer to do one or more of the following:

▶ Provide a down payment at the start of the project. This requirement is reasonable when the contractor needs to purchase a significant amount of materials and supplies during the early stages of the project.

▶ Make equal monthly payments based on the expected duration of the project. Cash outflow usually is smaller in the early stages of a project. If more cash is coming in than is going out during the early part of the project, the contractor may be able to invest some of the excess cash and earn interest. The saved funds can then be withdrawn to meet the greater cash outflow requirements later in the project.

▶ Provide frequent payments, such as weekly or monthly payments rather than quarterly payments.

The worst scenario from the contractor's point of view is to have the customer make only one payment at the end of the project. In this situation, the contractor will need to borrow money to have cash available to meet expenses throughout the project.

The contractor's outflow of cash can also be controlled by the terms of payment, in this case in contracts with suppliers. The contractor wants to delay payments (cash outflow) as long as possible. For example, a contractor who has ordered $100,000 worth of material would want to wait until it has all been delivered before paying the supplier. If the supplier's invoice states that it must be paid within thirty days, the contractor would probably hold off until about the 27th day before making the payment.

Project Management Software

Project management software makes it fairly easy to handle the cost considerations of a project. All costs associated with each resource in a project can be stored, and the software will calculate the budget for each work package and for the entire project. It will calculate the actual costs as the project proceeds and will forecast the final costs, as well. Because various resources have different rate structures and charge their rates at various points in the project, project management software usually allows the user to define different rate structures for each resource and when charges for those resources will actually be accrued.

At any time during a project, cost estimates, allocated total budgeted cost, cumulative budgeted cost, actual cost, earned value, committed costs, a cost performance index, cost variance, and a cost forecast can be calculated for each task, each work package, or the entire project, with a click of the mouse. Cost tables and graphs are often available to help analyze cost performance.

CHAPTER 8

Life-Cycle Costing and Target Costing

Life-cycle costing tracks and accumulates all product costs in the value chain from research and development and design of products and processes through production, marketing, distribution, and customer service. The value chain is the set of activities required to design, develop, produce, market, and service a product (or service). The terms "cradle-to-grave costing" and "womb-to tomb" costing" conveys the sense of fully capturing all costs associated with the product.

It focuses on minimizing locked-in costs, for example, by reducing the number of parts, promoting standardization of parts, and using equipment that can make more than one kind of product. The product life cycle is simply the time a product exists—from conception to abandonment. *Life-cycle costs* are all costs associated with the product for its entire life cycle. These costs include development (planning, design, and testing), manufacturing (conversion activities), and logistics support (advertising, distribution, warranty, and so on).

Because total customer satisfaction has become a vital issue in the new business setting, whole-life cost has emerged as the central focus of life-cycle cost management. *Whole-life cost* is the life-cycle cost of a product plus after-purchase (or post-purchase) costs that consumers incur, including operation, support, maintenance, and disposal. Since the costs a purchaser incurs after buying a product can be a significant percentage of whole-life costs and, thus, an important consideration in the purchase decision, managing activities so that whole-life costs are reduced can provide an important competitive advantage. Notice that cost reduction not cost control is the emphasis.

Moreover, cost reduction is achieved by judicious analysis and management of activities. Whole-life costing emphasizes management of the entire value chain. Thus, life-cycle cost management focuses on managing value-chain activities so that a long-term competitive advantage is created. To achieve this goal, managers must balance a product's whole-life cost, method of delivery innovativeness, and various product attributes including performance, features offered, reliability, conformance, durability, aesthetics, and perceived quality.

Cost Reduction

Studies show that 90 percent or more of a product's costs are committed during the development stage. Thus, it makes sense to emphasize management of activities during this phase of a product's existence. Every dollar spent on premanufacturing activities is known to save $8-$10 on manufacturing and postmanufacturing activities. The real opportunities for cost reduction occur before manufacturing begins. Managers need to invest more in premanufacturing assets and dedicate more resources to activities in the early phases of the product life cycle so that overall whole-life costs can be reduced.

The traditional emphasis has been on controlling costs *during* the production stage (when much less can be done to influence them). Furthermore, product cost has been narrowly defined as production costs; development and logistics costs have been treated as period costs and have been virtually ignored when computing product profitability Additionally, little attention has been given to the effect of the customer's after-purchase (or post-purchase) costs. Other costs that traditional methods ignore are the after-purchase costs (operating, support, repair, and disposal) incurred by customers. Accordingly, whole-life cost is a concept closely associated with life-cycle cost.

Whole-life Product Cost

Whole-life cost equals the life-cycle cost plus after-purchase costs. Attention to the reduction of all whole-life costs through analysis and management of all value-chain activities is a powerful competitive tool because of the potential for increasing customer satisfaction. From a whole-life point of view, product cost is made up of four major elements (1) nonrecurring development costs (planning, designing, and testing), (2) manufacturing costs, (3) logistic costs, and (4) the customer's after-purchase costs. Measuring, accumulating, and reporting all of a product's whole-life costs allow managers to better assess the effectiveness of life-cycle planning and build more effective and sophisticated marketing strategies. Life-cycle costing also increases their ability to make good pricing decisions and improve the assessment of product profitability.

Role of Target Costing

Life-cycle and whole-life cost concepts are associated with target costing and target pricing. A firm may determine that market conditions require that a product sell at a given target price. Hence, target cost can be determined by subtracting the desired unit profit margin from the target price. The cost reduction objectives of life-cycle and whole-life cost management can therefore be determined using target costing.

Thus, *target costing* (to be discussed in detail later) becomes a particularly useful tool for establishing cost reduction goals. Toyota, for example, calculates the lifetime target profit for a new car model by multiplying a target profit ratio times the target sales. They then calculate the estimated profit by subtracting the estimated costs from target sales. Usually, (at this point), target profit is greater than estimated profit. The cost reduction goal is defined by the difference between the target profit and the estimated profit. Toyota then searches for cost reduction opportunities through better design of the new model. Toyota's management recognizes that more opportunities exit for cost reduction during product planning than in actual development and production.

Example 1

YHY Company produces electronic products that typically have about a twenty-seven-month life cycle. At the beginning of the last quarter of 20x7, a new component was proposed. Design engineering believed that the product would be ready to produce by the beginning of 20x8. To produce this and other similar products, resistors had to be inserted into a circuit board. Management had discovered that the cost of the circuit board was driven by the number of insertions. Knowing this, design engineering produced the new component using fewer insertions than used by products in the past.

The budgeted costs and profits for the product over its two-year life cycle are illustrated in Exhibit 25. Notice that the life-cycle unit cost is $8 per unit compared with the conventional definition of $6 (which includes only the production costs) and the whole-life cost of $10. To be viable, of course, the product must cover all of its life-cycle costs and produce an acceptable profit. The $14 price was set with this objective in mind. Focusing only on the $6 cost could have led to a suboptimal pricing decision. Changing the focus requires managers to move away from the traditional, financially driven definition of product cost. Conventional cost systems do not directly identify development costs with the product being developed. The whole-life cost provides even more information—information that could prove vital for the company's life-cycle strategy. For example, if competitors sell a similar product for the same price but with after-purchase costs of only $1 per unit, the company could be at a competitive disadvantage. Given this information, actions can be considered that can eliminate the disadvantage (e.g., redesign of the product to lower the after-purchase cost).

Exhibit 25: Life-Cycle Costing: Budgeted Costs and Income

Unit Cost and Price Information

Unit manufacturing cost	$6
Unit logistics cost	2
Unit life-cycle cost	8
Unit after-purchase cost	2
Unit whole-life cost	10
Budgeted unit selling price	14

Budgeted Costs

Item	2x08	2x09	2x10	Item Total
Development costs	$195,000			$195,000
Manufacturing costs		240,000	360,000	600,000
Logistics costs		80,000	120,000	200,000
Annual subtotal	$195,000	$320,000	$480,000	$995,000
After-purchase costs		80,000	120,000	200,000
Annual total	$195,000	$400,000	$600,000	$1,195,000
Units produced		40,000	60,000	

Budgeted Product Income Statements

Year	Revenues	Costs	Annual Income	Cumulative Income
2x08		$195,000	-195,000	-195,000
2x09	$560,000	320,000	240,000	45,000
2x10	$840,000	480,000	360,000	405,000

Note: The post-purchase costs are costs incurred by the customer and so would not be included in the budgeted income statements.

Exhibit 26: Performance Report: Life-Cycle Costs

Year	Item	Actual Costs	Budgeted Costs	Variance
2x08	Development	$190,000	$195,000	$5,000 F
2x09	Production	300,000	240,000	(60,000) U
	Logistics	75,000	80,000	5,000 F
2x10	Production	435,000	360,000	(75,000) U
	Logistics	110,000	120,000	10,000 F

Analysis: Production costs were higher than expected because insertions of diodes and integrated circuits also drive costs (both production and post-purchase costs).
Conclusion: The design of future products should try to minimize total insertions.

Feedback on the effectiveness of life-cycle planning is also helpful. This information can help future new product planning as well as be useful for assessing how design decisions affect operational and support costs. Comparing actual costs with the budgeted costs can provide useful insights. Exhibit 26 illustrates a simple life-cycle cost performance report. As can be seen, production costs were greater than expected. Investigation revealed that costs are driven by total number of insertions, not just insertions of resistors. Further analysis also revealed that by reducing the total number of insertions, after-purchase costs could be reduced. Thus, future design work on similar products can benefit by the assessment.

Life-cycle Budget

A life-cycle budget estimates a product's revenues and expenses over its entire life cycle beginning with research and development, proceeding through the introduction and growth stages, into the maturity stage, and finally into the harvest or decline stage. This approach is especially useful when revenues and related costs do not occur in the same periods. It emphasizes the need to budget revenues to cover all costs, not just those for production. Hence, costs are determined for all value-chain categories: upstream (R&D, design), manufacturing, and downstream (marketing, distribution, and customer service). The result is to highlight upstream and downstream costs that often receive insufficient attention. Life-cycle budgeting adopts a life-cycle cost approach. This cost information is important for pricing decisions because revenues must cover costs incurred in each stage of the value chain, not just production.

Life-cycle budgeting emphasizes the relationships among costs incurred at different value-chain stages, for example, the effect of reduced design costs on future customer-service costs. Thus, life-cycle budgeting highlights the potential for locking in (designing in) future costs because the opportunity for cost reduction is greatest during the preproduction stages in the value chain.

Does the Product Add Value to the Company and to your Customer?

The value chain concept of the business functions is used to demonstrate how to use life-cycle costing to add value to organizations (see Exhibit 27). The *value chain* describes the linked set of activities that increase time usefulness (or value) of the products or services of an organization (value-added activities). Activities are evaluated by how they contribute to the final product's service, quality, and cost. In general, the business functions include the following:

▶ *Research and development*: The generation and development of ideas related to new products, services, or processes.

▶ *Design*: The detailed planning and engineering of products, services, or processes.

▶ *Production*: The aggregation and assembly of resources to produce a product or deliver a service.

▶ *Marketing*: The process that (a) informs potential customers about the attributes of products or services and (b) leads to the purchase of those products or services.

▶ *Distribution*: The mechanism established to deliver products or services to customers.

▶ *Customer service*: The product or service support activities provided to customers.

A *strategy and administration* function spans all the business activities described. Human resource management, tax planning, and legal matters, for example, potentially affect every step of the value chain. Life-cycle costing is a major means of helping managers to (a) run each of the business functions and (b) coordinate their activities within the framework of the entire organization.

Exhibit 27: The Value Chain of the Business Functions

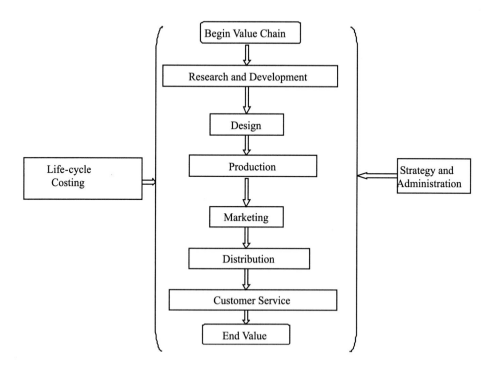

Target Costing

Target costing was developed by the Japanese to enhance their ability to compete in the global marketplace. Pricing based on target costing differs significantly from the conventional cost-based methods. Instead of first determining the cost of a product or service and then adding a profit factor to arrive at its price, target costing reverses the procedure.

Target costing is a pricing method that involves:

(1) Identifying the price at which a product will be competitive in the marketplace

(2) Defining the desired profit to be made on the product, and

(3) Computing the target cost for the product by subtracting the desired profit from the competitive market price.

The formula is:

$$\text{Target Price - Desired Profit} = \text{Target Cost}$$

Target cost is then given to the engineers and product designers, who use it as the maximum cost to be incurred for the materials and other resources needed to design and manufacture the product. It is their responsibility to create the product at or below its target cost.

Sometimes the engineers will determine that the product cannot be manufactured at or below its target cost. In that case, the product's design should be examined and attempts should be made to improve the approach to production. If the product still cannot be made at its target cost, the company must understand that its current facilities prevent it from competing in that particular market. The company should either invest in new equipment and procedures or abandon its plans to make and market the product.

One of the primary benefits of using target costing is the ability to design and build a product to a specific cost goal. The increased emphasis on product design allows the company to engineer the target cost into the product before manufacturing begins. A new product is designed only if its projected costs are equal to or lower than its target cost. Then, cost control efforts can focus on the committed cost curve, that is, on holding costs down in the planning and design stages, before the costs are actually committed and eventually incurred. Under the cost-based approach, concern about reducing costs begins only after the product has been produced. This often leads to random efforts to cut costs, which can reduce product quality and further erode the customer base.

In a highly competitive market, product quality and price determine which organizations will succeed. Customers will purchase the product that has the highest quality at the lowest price. The two variables—quality and price—go together; one cannot be sacrificed for the other. Target costing is a very useful pricing tool in such an environment because it allows an organization to critically analyze a product's potential for success before committing resources to its production. If an organization first manufactures a product and then finds out that its cost-based price is not competitive, the organization will lose the money it has already spent on the resources used to create the product. In most cases, the target costing approach can identify the potential success or failure of a product before many resources are spent on its creation.

Example 2

Lexus, a relative upstart with less than a fifth of Mercedes' 100-year history, sprinted past Mercedes sales three years ago and has been widening the gap ever since. The key is that a lot of Lexus customers might have been Mercedes buyers had the Japanese company not been so successful with its pricing strategy. Mercedes was dominated by engineers and used cost-based pricing.

When Lexus entered the U.S. market, it inverted the approach and used pricing based on target costing. The company decided to sell a high-quality luxury car for $38,000–about $10,000 less than the comparable Mercedes at the time–and then built the car to fit the price. Lexus was a marketing success. Mercedes was an engineering success but marketing failure.

Example 3

To see how target costing differs from the cost-based methods used for pricing decisions, consider Amber Furniture, Inc. Assume that the managers at Amber have made the strategic decision to expand the product line to offer a product that can compete with those offered by high-quality furniture manufacturers. The first piece in the new line is a bedroom chest of drawers, HY-107, constructed from clear (knot-free) pine and solid brass drawer pulls.

Amber's managers have invested resources in engineering drawings, product proto types, and studies of manufacturing processes before implementing full-scale production of the HY-107. Naturally they want to recover that investment and earn a profit on the sale of the new product. To determine the price of the HY-107, the cost accountants estimate the per-unit costs of producing the chest, as shown in Exhibit 28.

Amber's cost accountants offered the following explanation of the unit costs:

Direct materials. The HY-107 chest differs from other products in the line because expensive, knot-free wood and solid brass are used in its construction.

Exhibit 28: Unit Cost

Direct materials		
	Pine lumber	$90
	Brass drawer pulls	55
	Stain/polyurethane	4
Direct labor:		
	Cutting	25
	Assembly	40
	Finishing	30
Factory overhead:		
	Cutting	30
	Assembly	90
	Finishing	76
Total manufacturing cost		$440
Estimated selling and administrative expenses		$25
Total cost per unit		$465

Direct labor. Cost accountants predict that the direct labor costs of the HY-107 in the cutting department will be identical to that of other products in the line. However, they expect direct labor costs to go up in the assembly and finishing departments because the process of assembling and finishing the HY-107 chest is more complicated and time-consuming than for other products in the line.

Factory overhead. The increase in the manufacturing costs per unit of the HY-107 chest is in large part due to additional engineering time and new equipment purchased solely to assemble and finish the new chest.

Estimated selling and administrative expenses. The managers at Amber want to associate selling and administrative expenses directly with the HY-107 to understand the full cost of manufacturing and delivering a unit of product. These direct costs include salespersons' commissions and various administrative expenses.

To ensure the highest quality assembly and finishing, management decides to market the HY-107 exclusively in finished form through specialty furniture stores. The total estimated cost of the HY-107 is $465. Amber generally adds a 25% markup to the unit cost when it quotes prices to customers. Thus, the markup dollar amount for Amber is calculated as follows:

Unit cost x 0.25 = markup

The managers at Amber calculate the selling price to a furniture store as follows:

(Unit manufacturing cost + selling and administrative expenses) x markup percentage = markup in dollars

$$(\$440.00 + \$25.00) \times 0.25 = \$116.25$$

Unit manufacturing cost + selling and administrative expenses + markup in dollars = selling price

$$\$440.00 + \$25.00 + \$116.25 = \$581.25$$

Using costs to help them determine a selling price, Amber's managers set the wholesale price of the chest at $582. After applying their own markup, retailers must sell the chest for approximately $950. Unfortunately, after producing a new catalog and price list, as well as floor models of the HY-107 for display in retailers' showrooms, the managers at Amber hear some disappointing news. Retailers are not interested in carrying the line because consumers are not willing to pay $950 retail for pine furniture, even when that furniture is constructed of knot-free lumber and solid brass pulls.

This situation illustrates a traditional cost-based pricing policy in which the following steps occur:
1. A product and manufacturing process are designed.
2. The product is manufactured.
3. Manufacturing costs are accumulated.
4. The unit cost plus markup determines the selling price.
5. The company tries to sell the product.

What's missing here is an analysis of the market and an understanding of what consumers want. Although the new chest seemed to meet consumers' demands for quality and functionality, it did not meet their price demands. By starting the pricing process with their costs, Amber's managers priced the HY-107 out of its market.

Target costing changes the focus of the pricing decision: Instead of cost determining the selling price, the selling price determines costs. The purpose of a *target costing* system is to provide quality and functionality at a cost that achieves long-term profit objectives. The target here isn't the selling price; it's the cost at which a product of a certain quality and functionality can be produced.

The process is simple:
1. Determine the quality and functionality consumers want in a new product and the price they are willing to pay for that product.
2. Subtract the manufacturer's margin from the price to determine what the manufacture can spend to produce the product.
3. Study the feasibility of the new product. Can the company produce a product consumers want at a price the market will accept?

The target-cost calculation involves an understanding of the relationships among three variables: the selling price, the targeted manufacturing cost (cost), and the required margin. The relationship among the variables is defined as follows:

Target price – Desired profit = Target cost

Suppose that market research sets the wholesale price of the HY-107 at $380. Management has determined a margin of 22% on sales is required for long-term profitability. The company's required margin and target cost are calculated as follows:

selling price x 0.22 = margin

margin = $380 x 0.22 = $83.6

The target-cost information for Amber can be summarized as follows:

Selling price	$380
Less required margin	83.6
Target cost	$296.4

Exhibit 29 compares the cost plus philosophy with the target costing philosophy.

Exhibit 29: Cost-plus Pricing versus Target Costing

	FORMULA	IMPLICATIONS
Cost-plus pricing	Cost base + markup = selling price	• Cost is the base (given) • Markup is added (given) • The firm puts the product on the market and hopes the selling price is accepted
Pricing based on target costing	Target selling price – Desired profit = Target cost	• Markets determine prices (given) • Desired profit must be sustained for survival (given) • Target cost is the residual, the variable to be managed

Determining the cost at which Amber must deliver the HY-107 is the first step in using target costing for strategic purposes. Clearly the managers at Amber have a problem: To market the new chest successfully, they have to reduce the unit cost of producing the chest from $465 to $296.4.

One way companies begin to address a cost problem is by forming a multidisciplinary team, a team whose members are drawn from different functions—marketing, accounting, finance, production, purchasing, and engineering, for example. The team looks for ways to save costs and to eliminate inefficiencies. An understanding of cost behavior is a key to understanding the cost-effectiveness of design changes in products and manufacturing processes.

Amber's team would evaluate the major cost categories— manufacturing and selling and administrative *or* variable or fixed. Its managers would discuss redesigning the manufacturing process, reconsidering the types of materials used and ways to reduce suppliers' costs. They would study the sources of overhead costs and methods of reducing those costs. Based on the team's recommendations, Amber's top management may decide to manufacture the HY-107 or drop the product from further consideration.

Example 4

A salesperson at Milmool Products Company has reported that a customer is seeking price quotations for two electronic components: a special-purpose battery charger (Product X101) and a small transistorized machine computer (Product Y101). Competing for the customer's order are one French company and two Japanese companies. The current market price ranges for the two products are as follows:

> Product X101 $310—$370 per unit
>
> Product Y101 $720—$820 per unit

The salesperson feels that if Milmool could quote prices of $325 for Product X101 and $700 for Product Y101, the company would get the order and gain a significant share of the global market for those goods. Milmool's usual profit markup is 25 percent of total unit cost. The company's design engineers and cost accountants put together the following specifications and costs for the new products:

Activity-based cost rates:

Materials handling activity	$1.30 per dollar of raw materials and purchased parts cost
Production activity	$3.50 per machine hour
Product delivery activity	$24.00 per unit of X101
	$30.00 per unit of Y101

	Product X101	Product Y101
Projected unit demand	26,000	18,000
Per unit data:		
Raw materials cost	$30.00	$65.00
Purchased parts cost	$15.00	$45.00
Manufacturing labor		
Hours	2.6	4.8
Hourly labor rate	$12.00	$15.00
Assembly labor		
Hours	3.4	8.2
Hourly labor rate	$14.00	$16.00
Machine hours	12.8	28.4

The company wants to address the following three questions:

1. What is the target cost for each product?
2. What is the projected total unit cost of production and delivery?
3. Using the target costing approach, should the company produce the products?

1.   Target cost for each product:

$$\text{Product X101} = \$325.00 \div 1.25 = \$260.00^*$$

$$\text{Product Y101} = \$700.00 \div 1.25 = \$560.00$$

*Target Price - Desired Profit = Target Cost

$$\$325.00 - .25X = X$$

$$\$325.00 = 1.25X$$

$$X = \frac{\$325.00}{1.25} = \$260.00$$

1.   Projected total unit cost of production arid delivery:

	Product X101	Product Y101
Raw materials cost	$ 30.00	$ 65.00
Purchased parts cost	15.00	45.00
Total cost of raw materials and parts	$ 45.00	$110.00
Manufacturing labor		
X101 (2.6 hours X $12.00)	31.20	
Y101 (4.8 hours x $15.00)		72.00
Assembly labor		
X101 (3.4 hours X $14.00)	47.60	
Y101 (8.2 hours X $16.00)		131.20
Activity-based costs		
Materials handling activity		
X101 ($45.00 x $1.30)	58.500	
Y101 ($110.00 x $1.30)		143.00
Production activity		
X101 (12.8 machine hours x $3.50)	44.80	
Y101 (28.4 machine hours X $3.50)		99.40
Product delivery activity		
X101	24.00	
Y101		30.00
Projected total unit cost	$251.10	$585.60

3.   Production decision:

	PRODUCT X101	PRODUCT Y101
Target unit cost	$260.00	$560.00
Less: projected unit cost	251.10	585.60
Difference	$8.90	($25.60)

Product X101 can be produced below its target cost, so it should be produced. As currently designed, Product Y101 cannot be produced at or below its target cost; either it needs to be redesigned or the company should drop plans to make it.

CHAPTER 9

Economic Feasibility Study for a Capital Investment Project

Capital budgeting is the process of making long-term decisions for alternative investment opportunities. There are many investment decisions that a company may have to make in order to grow. Examples of capital budgeting applications include installation of a new information system (IS), new product development, product line selection, and the keeping or selling of a business segment. A careful cost-benefit analysis must be performed to determine a project's economic feasibility.

What Are the Types of Investment Projects?

There are typically two types of long-term capital expenditure decisions:

1. *Selection decisions* regarding obtaining new facilities or expanding existing ones. Examples of such decisions may include:

    (a) Investments in property, plant, and equipment, as well as other types of assets.

    (b) Resource commitments in the form of new product development and introduction of an information technology (IT) system.

    (c) Mergers and acquisitions in the form of buying another company to add a new product line.

2. *Replacement decisions* regarding the replacement of existing facilities with new ones. One example might be replacing an old machine with a newer, high-tech machine.

What Are the Features of Investment Projects?

Long-term investments have three important features:

1. They typically involve a large amounts of initial cash outlays which tend to have a long-term impact on the firm's future profitability. Therefore, this initial cash outlay needs to be justified on a cost-benefit basis.

2. There are expected recurring cash inflows (for example, increased revenues, savings in cash operating expenses, etc.) over the life of the investment project. This frequently requires consideration of the **time value of money**.

3. Income taxes can make a difference in the accept- or reject-decision. Therefore, income tax factors must be taken into account in every capital budgeting decision.

Understanding the Concept of Time Value of Money

"A dollar now is worth more than a dollar later." This statement sums up an important principle: money has a time value. The essence of this principle is not to suggest that inflation might make the dollar worth less if received at a later point in time. It merely implies that a dollar now can be invested so that you have more than a dollar at any later time.

Time value of money is a critical consideration in financial and investment decisions. For example, compound interest calculations are needed to determine future sums of money resulting from an investment. Discounting, or the calculation of present value, is inversely related to compounding, which is used to evaluate the future cash flow associated with capital budgeting projects. There are plenty of applications of time value of money in accounting and finance.

How Do You Calculate Future Values – How Money Grows?

A dollar in hand today is worth more than a dollar to be received tomorrow because of the interest it could earn from putting it in a savings account or placing it in an investment account. Compounding interest means that interest earns interest. For the discussion of the concepts of compounding and time value, let us define:

F_n = future value: the amount of money at the end of year n

P = principal

i = annual interest rate

n = number of years

Then,

F_1 = the amount of money at the end of year 1

= principal and interest = $P + iP = P(1+i)$

F_2 = the amount of money at the end of year 2

= $F_1(1+i) = P(1+i)(1+i) = P(1+i)^2$

If we continued to n years, the future value of an investment compounded annually at rate i for n years is

$F_n = P(1+i)^n = P \cdot T1(i,n)$

where T1(i,n) is the compound amount of $1 and can be found in Table 1.

Example 1

You place $1,000 in a savings account earning 8 percent interest compounded annually. How much money will you have in the account at the end of 4 years?

$F_n = P(1+i)^n$

F_4 = $1,000 (1 + 0.08)^4 = $1,000\ T1(8\%, 4\ \text{years})$

From Table 1, the T1 for 4 years at 8 percent is 1.361.

Therefore, F_4 = $1,000 (1.361) = $1,361.

Example 2

You invested a large sum of money in the stock of Delta Corporation. The company paid a $3 dividend per share. The dividend is expected to increase by 20 percent per year for the next 3 years. You wish to project the dividends for years 1 through 3.

$$F_n = P(1+i)^n$$

$$F_1 = \$3(1+0.2)^1 = \$3\,T1(20\%,1) = \$3\,(1.200) = \$3.60$$

$$F_2 = \$3(1+0.2)^2 = \$3\,T1(20\%,2) = \$3\,(1.440) = \$4.32$$

$$F_3 = \$3(1+0.2)^3 = \$3\,T1(20\%,3) = \$3\,(1.728) = \$5.18$$

Future Value of an Annuity

An annuity is defined as a series of payments (or receipts) of a fixed amount for a specified number of periods. Each payment is assumed to occur at the end of the period. The future value of an annuity is a compound annuity which involves depositing or investing an equal sum of money at the end of each year for a certain number of years and allowing it to grow.

Let $\quad S_n$ = the future value on an n-year annuity

$\qquad$ A = the amount of an annuity

Then we can write

$$S_n = A(1+i)^{n-1} + A(1+i)^{n-2} + ... + A(1+i)^0$$

$$= A[(1+i)^{n-1}+(1+i)^{n-2}+ ... + (1+i)^0]$$

$$= A \cdot \sum_{t=0}^{n-1}(1+i)^t \qquad = A\left[\frac{(1+i)^n - 1}{i}\right] = A \cdot T2(i,n)$$

where T2(i,n) represents the future value of an annuity of $1 for n years compounded at i percent and can be found in Table 2.

Example 3

You wish to determine the sum of money you will have in a savings account at the end of 6 years by depositing $1,000 at the end of each year for the next 6 years. The annual interest rate is 8 percent. The T2(8%,6 years) is given in Table 2 as 7.336. Therefore,

$$S_6 = \$1,000\,T2(8\%,6) = \$1,000\,(7.336) = \$7,336$$

Example 4

You deposit $30,000 semiannually into a fund for ten years. The annual interest rate is 8 percent. The amount accumulated at the end of the tenth year is calculated as follows:

$$S_n = A.\,T2(i, n)$$

where $\quad$ A = $30,000

$\qquad$ i = 8%/2 = 4%

$\qquad$ n = 10 x 2 = 20

Then,

$$S_n = \$30,000 \, T2(4\%, 20)$$

$$= \$30,000 \, (29.778) = \$893,340$$

What Is Present Value - How Much Money Is Worth Now?

Present value is the present worth of future sums of money. The process of calculating present values, or discounting, is actually the opposite of finding the compounded future value. In connection with present value calculations, the interest rate i is called the *discount rate*. The discount rate we use is more commonly called the *cost of capital*, which is the minimum rate of return required by the investor.

Recall that $F_n = P(1+i)^n$

Then,
$$P = \frac{F_n}{(1+i)^n} = F_n \left[\frac{1}{(1+i)^n} \right] = F_n \cdot T3(i,n)$$

Where T3(i,n) represents the present value of $1 and is given in Table 3.

Example 5

You have been given an opportunity to receive $20,000 6 years from now. If you can earn 10 percent on your investments, what is the most you should pay for this opportunity? To answer this question, you must compute the present value of $20,000 to be received 6 years from now at a 10 percent rate of discount. F_6 is $20,000, I is 10 percent, and n is 6 years. T3(10%,6) from Table 3 is 0.565.

$$P = \$20,000 \left[\frac{1}{(1+0.1)^6} \right] = \$20,000 \, T3(10\%,6) = \$20,000(0.564) = \$11,280$$

This means that you can earn 10 percent on your investment, and you would be indifferent to receiving $11,280 now or $20,000 6 years from today since the amounts are time equivalent. In other words, you could invest $11,300 today at 10 percent and have $20,000 in 6 years.

Present Value of Mixed Streams of Cash Flows

The present value of a series of mixed payments (or receipts) is the sum of the present value of each individual payment. We know that the present value of each individual payment is the payment times the appropriate T3 value.

Example 6

You are thinking of starting a new product line that initially costs $32,000. Your annual projected cash inflows are:

1 $10,000

2 $20,000

3 $5,000

If you must earn a minimum of 10 percent on your investment, should you undertake this new product line?

The present value of this series of mixed streams of cash inflows is calculated as follows:

Year	Cash inflows	x T3(10%, n)	Present Value
1	$10,000	0.909	$9,090
2	$20,000	0.826	$16,520
3	$5,000	0.751	$3,755
			$29,365

Since the present value of your projected cash inflows is less than the initial investment, you should not undertake this project.

Present Value of an Annuity

Interest received from bonds, pension funds, and insurance obligations involve annuities. To compare these financial instruments, we need to know the present value of each. The present value of an annuity (P_n) can be found by using the following equation:

$$P_n = A \cdot \left[\frac{1}{(1+i)^1} \right] + A \cdot \left[\frac{1}{(1+i)^2} \right] + \cdots + A \cdot \left[\frac{1}{(1+i)^n} \right]$$

$$= A \cdot \left[\frac{1}{(1+i)^1} + \frac{1}{(1+i)^2} + \cdots + \frac{1}{(1+i)^n} \right]$$

$$= A \cdot \sum_{t=1}^{n} \frac{1}{(1+i)^t} = A \cdot \frac{1}{i} \left[1 - \frac{1}{(1+i)^n} \right]$$

$$= A \cdot T4(i,n)$$

where T4(i,n) represents the present value of an annuity of $1 discounted at i percent for n years and is found in Table 4.

Example 7

Assume that the cash inflows in Example 6 form an annuity of $10,000 for 3 years. Then the present value is

$$P_n = A \cdot T4(i,n)$$

$$P_3 = \$10,000 \, T4(10\%, 3 \text{ years}) = \$10,000 \, (2.487) = \$24,870$$

Use of Financial Calculators and Spreadsheet Programs

There are many financial calculators that contain pre-programmed formulas to perform many present value and future applications. They include various models from *Hewlett-Packard*, *Sharpe*, and *Texas Instrument*. Furthermore, spreadsheet software such as *Excel* has built-in financial functions to perform many such applications.

How Do You Measure Investment Worth?

Several methods of evaluating investment projects are as follows:
1. Payback period
2. Net present value (NPV)
3. Internal rate of return (IRR)
4. Weighted Scoring Model

The NPV method and the IRR method are called *discounted cash flow (DCF) methods*. Each of these methods is discussed below.

1. Payback Period

The payback period measures the length of time required to recover the amount of initial investment. It is computed by dividing the initial investment by the cash inflows through increased revenues or cost savings. It is also known as *time to money* or *breakeven period*.

Example 8

Assume:

Cost of investment	$18,000
Annual after-tax cash savings	$3,000

Then, the payback period is:

$$\text{Payback period} = \frac{\text{initial investment}}{\text{cost savings}} = \frac{\$18,000}{\$3,000} = 6 \text{ years}$$

Decision rule: Choose the project with the shorter payback period. The rationale behind this choice is: The shorter the payback period, the less risky the project, and the greater the liquidity.

Example 9

Consider the two projects whose after-tax cash inflows are not even. Assume each project costs $1,000.

Year	Cash Inflow A($)	B($)
1	100	500
2	200	400
3	300	300
4	400	100
5	500	
6	600	

When cash inflows are not even, the payback period has to be found by trial and error. The payback period of project A is ($1,000= $100 + $200 + $300 + $400) 4 years. The payback period of project B is $1,000 = $500 + $400 + $100):

$$2 \text{ years} + \frac{\$100}{\$300} = 2\frac{1}{3} \text{ years}$$

Project B is the project of choice in this case, since it has the shorter payback period.

The advantages of using the payback period method of evaluating an investment project are that (1) it is simple to compute and easy to understand, and (2) it handles investment risk effectively.

The shortcomings of this method are that (1) it does not recognize the time value of money, and (2) it ignores the impact of cash inflows received after the payback period; essentially, cash flows after the payback period determine profitability of an investment.

2. Net Present Value

Net present value (NPV) is the excess of the present value (PV) of cash inflows generated by the project over the amount of the initial investment (I):

$$NPV = PV - I$$

The present value of future cash flows is computed using the so-called cost of capital (or minimum required rate of return) as the discount rate. When cash inflows are uniform, the present value would be

$$PV = A . T4 (i, n)$$

where A is the amount of the annuity. The value of T4 is found in Table 4.

Decision rule: If NPV is positive, accept the project. Otherwise reject it.

Example 10

Consider the following investment:

Initial investment	$12,950
Estimated life	10 years
Annual cash inflows	$3,000
Cost of capital (minimum required rate of return)	12%

Present value of the cash inflows is:

$$PV = A.T4(i,n)$$
$$= \$3,000. T4(12\%,10 \text{ years})$$

= $3,000 (5.650)	$16,950
Initial investment (I)	12,950
Net present value (NPV = PV - I)	$4,000

Since the NPV of the investment is positive, the investment should be accepted.

The advantages of the NPV method are that it obviously recognizes the time value of money and it is easy to compute whether the cash flows form an annuity or vary from period to period.

3. Internal Rate of Return

Internal rate of return (IRR), also called *time adjusted rate of return,* is defined as the rate of interest that equates I with the PV of future cash inflows.

In other words,

$$\text{at IRR } I = PV \text{ or } NPV = 0$$

Decision rule: Accept the project if the IRR exceeds the cost of capital. Otherwise, reject it.

Example 11

Assume the same data given in Example 10, and set the following equality (I = PV):

$$\$12,950 = \$3,000 \cdot T4(i, 10 \text{ years})$$

$$T_4(i, 10 \text{ years}) = \frac{\$12,950}{\$3,000} = 4.317$$

which stands somewhere between 18 percent and 20 percent in the 10-year line of Table 4. The interpolation follows:

	PV of An Annuity of $1 Factor	
	T4(i,10 years)	
18%	4.494	4.494
IRR	4.317	
20%		4.192
Difference	0.177	0.302

Therefore,

$$IRR = 18\% + \frac{0.177}{0.302} \quad (20\% - 18\%)$$

$$= 18\% + 0.586(2\%) = 18\% + 1.17\% = 19.17\%$$

Since the IRR of the investment is greater than the cost of capital (12 percent), accept the project.

The advantage of using the IRR method is that it does consider the time value of money and, therefore, is more exact and realistic than the ARR method.

The shortcomings of this method are that (1) it is time-consuming to compute, especially when the cash inflows are not even, although most financial calculators and PCs have a key to calculate IRR, and (2) it fails to recognize the varying sizes of investment in competing projects.

Can A Computer Help?

Spreadsheet programs can be used in making IRR calculations. For example, *Excel* has a function IRR(values, guess). Excel considers negative numbers as cash outflows such as the initial investment, and positive numbers as cash inflows. Many financial calculators have similar features. As in Example 13, suppose you want to calculate the IRR of a $12,950 investment (the value --12950 entered in year 0 that is followed by 10 monthly cash inflows of $3,000). Using a guess of 12% (the value of 0.12), which is in effect the cost of capital, your formula would be @IRR(values, 0.12) and Excel would return 19.15%, as shown below.

Year 0	1	2	3	4	5	6	7	8	9	10
-12950	3000	3000	3000	3000	3000	3000	3000	3000	3000	3000

IRR =	19.15%
NPV =	$4,000.67

Note: The *Excel* formula for NPV is NPV (discount rate, cash inflow values) + I, where I is given as a negative number.

4. Weighted Scoring Model

A weighted scoring model is a tool that provides a systematic process for selecting projects based on many criteria. These criteria can focus on how to meet broad organizational needs or how to address problems, opportunities, and directives, or they can be factors such as the amount of time it will take to complete the project, the overall priority of the project, or the projected financial performance of the project.

The first step in creating a weighted scoring model is to identify criteria important to the project selection process. It often takes time to develop and reach agreement on these criteria. Holding facilitated brainstorming sessions or using groupware to exchange ideas can aid in the development of these criteria. Some possible criteria for information technology projects include:

- ▶ Support of key business objectives
- ▶ Strong internal sponsorship
- ▶ Strong customer support
- ▶ Use of realistic levels of technology
- ▶ Implementation in one year or less
- ▶ Positive net present value provided
- ▶ Low risk in meeting scope, time, and cost goals

Once the criteria have been identified, a weight should be assigned to each criterion individually. These weights indicate the value or importance of each criterion. You can assign weights based on percentages, in which case the total sum of all weights must equal 100 percent. You then assign numerical scores to each criterion (for example, 0 to 100) for each project. The scores indicate how much each project meets each criterion. At this point, you can use a spreadsheet application to create a matrix of projects, criteria, weights, and scores. Exhibit 29 provides an example of a weighted scoring model to evaluate four different projects. After assigning weights for the criteria and scores for each project, you calculate a weighted score for each project by multiplying the weight for each criterion by its score and adding the resulting values.

Exhibit 29: Sample Weighted Scoring Model for Project Selection— Using an Excel Spreadsheet

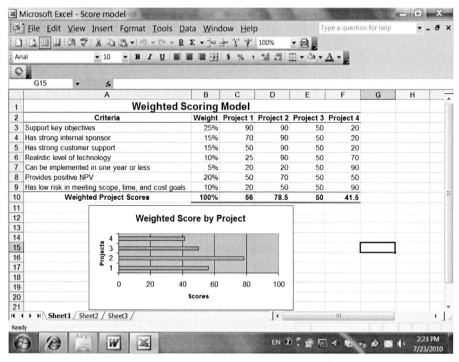

For example, you calculate the weighted score for Project 1 in Exhibit 29 as:

$$25\% * 90 + 15\% * 70 + 15\% * 50 + 10\% * 25 + 5\% * 20 + 20\% * 50 + 10\% * 20 = 56$$

Note that in this example, Project 2 would be the obvious choice for selection since it has the highest weighted score. Creating a bar chart to graph the weighted scores for each project allows you to see the results easily. Creating the weighted scoring model in a spreadsheet allows you to enter the data, create and copy formulas, and perform "what-if" analyses. For example, suppose you change the weights for the criteria. By having the weighted scoring model in a spreadsheet, you can easily change the weights, and the weighted scores and charts will be updated automatically.

You can also assign weights by providing points. For example, a project might receive 10 points if it definitely supports key business objectives, 5 points if it somewhat supports them, and 0 points if it is totally unrelated to key business objectives. With a point model, you can simply add all the points to determine the best projects for selection, without having to multiply weights and scores and sum the results. You can also determine minimum scores or thresholds for specific criteria in a weighted scoring model. For example, suppose a project really should not be considered if it does not score at least 50 out of 100 on every criterion. You can build this type of threshold into the weighted scoring model to reject projects that do not meet these minimum standards.

How Do Income Taxes Affect Investment Decisions?

Income taxes make a difference in many capital budgeting decisions. The project that seems most attractive on a before-tax basis may have to be rejected on an after-tax basis and vice versa. Income taxes typically affect both the amount and the timing of cash flows. Since net income, not cash inflows, is subject to tax, after-tax cash inflows are not usually the same as after-tax net income.

Income taxes typically affect both the amount and the timing of cash flows. Since net income, not cash inflows, is subject to tax, after-tax cash inflows are not usually the same as after-tax net income.

How to Calculate After-Tax Cash Flows

Let us define:

$$S = \text{Sales}$$

$$E = \text{Cash operating expenses}$$

$$d = \text{Depreciation}$$

$$t = \text{Tax rate}$$

Then, before-tax cash inflows (or cash savings) = S - E and net income = S - E - d
By definition,

After-tax cash inflows = Before-tax cash inflows - Taxes = (S - E) - (S - E - d) (t)

Rearranging gives the short-cut formula:

After-tax cash inflows $\quad= (S - E) (1 - t) + (d)(t)$ or

$$= (S - E - d) (1 - t) + d$$

The deductibility of depreciation from sales in arriving at taxable net income reduces income tax payments and thus serves as a *tax shield*.

Tax shield = Tax savings on depreciation = (d)(t)

Example 12

Assume:

$$S = \$12,000$$

$$E = \$10,000$$

$$d = \$500 \text{ per year using the straight line method}$$

$$t = 30\%$$

Then,

After-tax cash inflow $= (\$12,000 - \$10,000)(1 - .3) + (\$500)(.3)$

$= (\$2,000)(.7) + (\$500)(.3)$

$= \$1,400 + \$150 = \$1,550$

Note that a tax shield $= \text{tax savings on depreciation} = (d)(t)$

$= (\$500)(.3) = \$150$

Since the tax shield is dt, the higher the depreciation deduction, the higher the tax savings on depreciation. Therefore, an accelerated depreciation method (such as double-declining balance) produces higher tax savings than the straight-line method. Accelerated methods produce higher present values for the tax savings which may make a given investment more attractive.

Example 13

The Bechard Company estimates that it can save $2,500 a year in cash operating costs for the next ten years if it buys a special-purpose machine at a cost of $10,000. No residual value is expected. Depreciation is by straight-line. Assume that the income tax rate is 30%, and the after-tax cost of capital (minimum required rate of return) is 10%. After-tax cash savings can be calculated as follows:

Depreciation by straight-line is $10,000/10 = $1,000 per year. Thus,

After-tax cash savings $= (S - E)(1 - t) + (d)(t)$

$= \$2,500(1 - .3) + \$1,000(.3)$

$= \$1,750 + \$300 = \$2,050$

To see if this machine should be purchased, the net present value can be calculated.

$PV = \$2,050 \, T4(10\%, 10 \text{ years}) = \$2,050 \, (6.145) = \$12,597.25$

Thus, $NPV = PV - I = \$12,597.25 - \$10,000 = \$2,597.25$

Since NPV is positive, the machine should be bought.

Example 14

Gerritt Corporation has provided its revenues and cash operating costs (excluding depreciation) for the old and the new machine, as follows:

	REVENUE	ANNUAL CASH OPERATING COSTS	NET PROFIT BEFORE DEPRECIATION AND TAXES
Old machine	$150,000	$70,000	$80,000
New machine	$180,000	$60,000	$120,000

Assume that the annual depreciation of the old machine and the new machine will be $30,000 and $50,000, respectively. Assume further that the tax rate is 46%.

To arrive at net profit after taxes, we first have to deduct depreciation expense from the net profit before depreciation and taxes, as follows:

	NET PROFITS AFTER TAXES	ADD DEPRECIATION	AFTER-TAX CASH INFLOWS
Old machine	($80,000-$30,000)(1-0.46)=$27,000	$30,000	$57,000
New machine	($120,000-$50,000)(1-0.46)=$37,800	$50,000	$87,800

Subtracting the after-tax cash inflows of the old machine from the cash inflows of the new machine results in the relevant, or incremental, cash inflows for each year.

Therefore, in this example, the relevant or incremental cash inflows for each year are $87,800 - $57,000 = $30,800.

Alternatively, the incremental cash inflows after taxes can be computed, using the following simple formula:

After-tax incremental cash inflows $= $ (increase in revenues)(1-tax rate)

- (increase in cash charges)(1-tax rate)

+ (increase in depreciation expenses)(tax rate)

Example 15

Using the data in Example 14, after-tax incremental cash inflows for each year are:

Increase in revenue x (1-tax rate):	
($180,000-$150,000)(1-0.46)	$16,200
- Increase in cash charges x (1-tax rate):	
($60,000-$70,000)(1-0.46)	- (-5,400)
+ Increase in depreciation expense x	
tax rate: ($50,000-$30,000)(0.46)	9,200
	$30,800

How Does MACRS Affect Investment Decisions?

Although the traditional depreciation methods can be used for computing depreciation for book purposes, 1981 saw a new way of computing depreciation deductions for tax purposes. The current rule is called the *Modified Accelerated Cost Recovery System* (MACRS) rule, as enacted by Congress in 1981 and then modified somewhat in 1986 under the Tax Reform Act of 1986. This rule is characterized as follows:

1. It abandons the concept of useful life and accelerates depreciation deductions by placing all depreciable assets into one of eight age property classes. It calculates deductions, based on an allowable percentage of the asset's original cost (See Tables 5 and 6). *Note:* MACRS for assets with lives of 10 years or fewer is based on the 200%-declining-balance method of depreciation. Thus, an asset with a 3-year life would have a straight-line rate of 33-1/3%, or a double-declining-balance rate of 66-2/3%.

   With a shorter asset tax life than useful life, the company would be able to deduct depreciation more quickly and save more in income taxes in the earlier years, thereby making an investment more attractive. The rationale behind the system is that this way the government encourages the company to invest in facilities and increase its productive capacity and efficiency. (Remember that the higher d, the larger the tax shield (d)(t)).

2. Since the allowable percentages in Table 5 add up to 100%, there is no need to consider the salvage value of an asset in computing depreciation.

3. The company may elect the straight line method. The straight-line convention must follow what is called the *half-year convention*. This means that the company can deduct only half of the regular straight-line depreciation amount in the first year.

The reason for electing to use the MACRS optional straight-line method is that some firms may prefer to stretch out depreciation deductions using the straight-line method rather than to accelerate them. Those firms are the ones that are just starting out or have little or no income and wish to show more income on their income statements.

Example 16

Assume that a machine falls under a 3-year property class and costs $3,000 initially. The straight line option under MACRS differs from the traditional straight line method in that under this method the company would deduct only $500 depreciation in the first year and the fourth year ($3,000/3 years =$1,000; $1,000/2=$500). The table below compares the straight line with half-year convention with the MACRS.

Year	Straight line (half-year) Depreciation	Cost		MACRS %	MACRS Deduction
1	$500	$3,000	X	33.3%	$999
2	1,000	3,000	X	44.5	1,335
3	1,000	3,000	X	14.8	444
4	500	3,000	X	7.4	222
	$3,000				$3,000

Example 17

A machine costs $10,000. Annual cash inflows are expected to be $5,000. The machine will be depreciated using the MACRS rule and will fall under the 3-year property class. The cost of capital after taxes is 10%. The estimated life of the machine is 4 years. The salvage value of the machine at the end of the fourth year is expected to be $ 1,200. The tax rate is 30%.

The formula for computation of after-tax cash inflows (S - E)(1 - t)+ (d)(t) needs to be computed separately. The NPV analysis can be performed as follows:

		Present value factor @ 10%	Present value
Initial investment: $10,000		1.000	$(10,000.00)
(S- E)(1 -t)			
$5,000 (1 - .3) = $3,500 for 4 years		3.170(a)	$11,095.00

(d)(t): Year	Cost		MACRS %	d	(d)(t)		
1	$10,000	X	33.3%	$3,330	$999	.909(b)	908.09
2	$10,000	X	44.5	4,450	1,335	.826(b)	1,102.71
3	$10,000	X	14.8	1,480	444	.751(b)	333.44
4	$10,000	X	7.4	740	222	.683(b)	151.63
Salvage value:							
$1,200 in year 4: $1,200 (1 - .3) = $840(c)					.683(b)		573.72
Net present value (NPV)							$4,164.59

(a) T4(10%, 4 years) = 3.170 (from Table 4).
(b) T3 values obtained from Table 3.

(c) Any salvage value received under the MACRS rules is a *taxable gain* (the excess of the selling price over book value, $1,200 in this example), since the book value will be zero at the end of the life of the machine.

Since NPV = PV - I = $4,164.59 is positive, the machine should be bought.

Table: 1 Future Value of $1 = T1(i,n)

Periods	4%	6%	8%	10%	12%	14%	20%
1	1.040	1.060	1.080	1.100	1.120	1.140	1.200
2	1.082	1.124	1.166	1.210	1.254	1.300	1.440
3	1.125	1.191	1.260	1.331	1.405	1.482	1.728
4	1.170	1.263	1.361	1.464	1.574	1.689	2.074
5	1.217	1.338	1.469	1.611	1.762	1.925	2.488
6	1.265	1.419	1.587	1.772	1.974	2.195	2.986
7	1.316	1.504	1.714	1.949	2.211	2.502	3.583
8	1.369	1.594	1.851	2.144	2.476	2.853	4.300
9	1.423	1.690	1.999	2.359	2.773	3.252	5.160
10	1.480	1.791	2.159	2.594	3.106	3.707	6.192
11	1.540	1.898	2.332	2.853	3.479	4.226	7.430
12	1.601	2.012	2.518	3.139	3.896	4.818	8.916
13	1.665	2.133	2.720	3.452	4.364	5.492	10.699
14	1.732	2.261	2.937	3.798	4.887	6.261	12.839
15	1.801	2.397	3.172	4.177	5.474	7.138	15.407
16	1.873	2.540	3.426	4.595	6.130	8.137	18.488
17	1.948	2.693	3.700	5.055	6.866	9.277	22.186
18	2.026	2.854	3.996	5.560	7.690	10.575	26.623
19	2.107	3.026	4.316	6.116	8.613	12.056	31.948
20	2.191	3.207	4.661	5.728	9.646	13.743	38.338
30	3.243	5.744	10.063	17.450	29.960	50.950	237.380
40	4.801	10.286	21.725	45.260	93.051	188.880	1469.800

Table 2: Future Value of an Annuity of $1 = T2(i,n)

Periods	4%	6%	8%	10%	12%	14%	20%
1	1.000	1.000	1.000	1.000	1.000	1.000	1.000
2	2.040	2.060	2.080	2.100	2.120	2.140	2.200
3	3.122	3.184	3.246	3.310	3.374	3.440	3.640
4	4.247	4.375	4.506	4.641	4.779	4.921	5.368
5	5.416	5.637	5.867	6.105	6.353	6.610	7.442
6	6.633	6.975	7.336	7.716	8.115	8.536	9.930
7	7.898	8.394	8.923	9.487	10.089	10.730	12.916
8	9.214	9.898	10.637	11.436	12.300	13.233	16.499
9	10.583	11.491	12.488	13.580	14.776	16.085	20.799
10	12.006	13.181	14.487	15.938	17.549	19.337	25.959
11	13.486	14.972	16.646	18.531	20.655	23.045	32.150
12	15.026	16.870	18.977	21.385	24.133	37.271	39.580
13	16.627	18.882	21.495	24.523	28.029	32.089	48.497
14	18.292	21.015	24.215	27.976	32.393	37.581	59.196
15	20.024	23.276	27.152	31.773	37.280	43.842	72.035
16	21.825	25.673	30.324	35.950	42.753	50.980	87.442
17	23.698	28.213	33.750	40.546	48.884	59.118	105.930
18	25.645	30.906	37.450	45.600	55.750	68.394	128.120
19	27.671	33.760	41.446	51.160	63.440	78.969	154.740
20	29.778	36.778	45.762	57.276	75.052	91.025	186.690
30	56.085	79.058	113.283	164.496	241.330	356.790	1181.900
40	95.026	154.762	259.057	442.597	767.090	1342.000	7343.900

*Payments (or receipts) at the *end* of each period.

Table 3: Present Value of $1 = T3(i,n)

PERIODS	3%	4%	5%	6%	7%	8%	10%	12%	14%	16%	18%	20%	22%	24%	25%	26%	28%	30%	40%
1	.9709	.9615	.9524	.9434	.9346	.9259	.9091	.8929	.8772	.8621	.8475	.8333	.8197	.8065	.8000	.7937	.7813	.7692	.7143
2	.9426	.9246	.9070	.8900	.8734	.8573	.8264	.7972	.7695	.7432	.7182	.6944	.6719	.6504	.6400	.6299	.6104	.5917	.5102
3	.9151	.8890	.8638	.8396	.8163	.7938	.7513	.7118	.6750	.6407	.6086	.5787	.5507	.5245	.5120	.4999	.4768	.4552	.3644
4	.8885	.8548	.8227	.7921	.7629	.7350	.6830	.6355	.5921	.5523	.5158	.4823	.4514	.4230	.4096	.3968	.3725	.3501	.2603
5	.8626	.8219	.7835	.7473	.7130	.6806	.6209	.5674	.5194	.4761	.4371	.4019	.3700	.3411	.3277	.3149	.2910	.2693	.1859
6	.8375	.7903	.7462	.7050	.6663	.6302	.5645	.5066	.4556	.4104	.3704	.3349	.3033	.2751	.2621	.2499	.2274	.2072	.1328
7	.8131	.7599	.7107	.6651	.6227	.5835	.5132	.4523	.3996	.3538	.3139	.2791	.2486	.2218	.2097	.1983	.1776	.1594	.0949
8	.7894	.7307	.6768	.6274	.5820	.5403	.4665	.4039	.3506	.3050	.2660	.2326	.2038	.1789	.1678	.1574	.1388	.1226	.0678
9	.7664	.7026	.6446	.5919	.5439	.5002	.4241	.3606	.3075	.2630	.2255	.1938	.1670	.1443	.1342	.1249	.1084	.0943	.0484
10	.7441	.6756	.6139	.5584	.5083	.4632	.3855	.3220	.2697	.2267	.1911	.1615	.1369	.1164	.1074	.0992	.0847	.0725	.0346
11	.7224	.6496	.5847	.5268	.4751	.4289	.3505	.2875	.2366	.1954	.1619	.1346	.1122	.0938	.0859	.0787	.0662	.0558	.0247
12	.7014	.6246	.5568	.4970	.4440	.3971	.3186	.2567	.2076	.1685	.1372	.1122	.0920	.0757	.0687	.0625	.0517	.0429	.0176
13	.6810	.6006	.5303	.4688	.4150	.3677	.2897	.2292	.1821	.1452	.1163	.0935	.0754	.0610	.0550	.0496	.0404	.0330	.0126
14	.6611	.5775	.5051	.4423	.3878	.3405	.2633	.2046	.1597	.1252	.0985	.0779	.0618	.0492	.0440	.0393	.0316	.0254	.0090
15	.6419	.5553	.4810	.4173	.3624	.3152	.2394	.1827	.1401	.1079	.0835	.0649	.0507	.0397	.0352	.0312	.0247	.0195	.0064
16	.6232	.5339	.4581	.3936	.3387	.2919	.2176	.1631	.1229	.0930	.0708	.0541	.0415	.0320	.0281	.0248	.0193	.0150	.0046
17	.6050	.5134	.4363	.3714	.3166	.2703	.1978	.1456	.1078	.0802	.0600	.0451	.0340	.0258	.0225	.0197	.0150	.0116	.0033
18	.5874	.4936	.4155	.3503	.2959	.2502	.1799	.1300	.0946	.0691	.0508	.0376	.0279	.0208	.0180	.0156	.0118	.0089	.0023
19	.5703	.4746	.3957	.3305	.2765	.2317	.1635	.1161	.0829	.0596	.0431	.0313	.0229	.0168	.0144	.0124	.0092	.0068	.0017
20	.5537	.4564	.3769	.3118	.2584	.2145	.1486	.1037	.0728	.0514	.0365	.0261	.0187	.0135	.0115	.0098	.0072	.0053	.0012
21	.5375	.4388	.3589	.2942	.2415	.1987	.1351	.0926	.0638	.0443	.0309	.0217	.0154	.0109	.0092	.0078	.0056	.0040	.0009
22	.5219	.4220	.3418	.2775	.2257	.1839	.1228	.0826	.0560	.0382	.0262	.0181	.0126	.0088	.0074	.0062	.0044	.0031	.0006
23	.5067	.4057	.3256	.2618	.2109	.1703	.1117	.0738	.0491	.0329	.0222	.0151	.0103	.0071	.0059	.0049	.0034	.0024	.0004
24	.4919	.3901	.3101	.2470	.1971	.1577	.1015	.0659	.0431	.0284	.0188	.0126	.0085	.0057	.0047	.0039	.0027	.0018	.0003
25	.4776	.3751	.2953	.2330	.1842	.1460	.0923	.0588	.0378	.0245	.0160	.0105	.0069	.0046	.0038	.0031	.0021	.0014	.0002
26	.4637	.3607	.2812	.2198	.1722	.1352	.0839	.0525	.0331	.0211	.0135	.0087	.0057	.0037	.0030	.0025	.0016	.0011	.0002
27	.4502	.3468	.2678	.2074	.1609	.1252	.0763	.0469	.0291	.0182	.0115	.0073	.0047	.0030	.0024	.0019	.0013	.0008	.0001
28	.4371	.3335	.2551	.1956	.1504	.1159	.0693	.0419	.0255	.0157	.0097	.0061	.0038	.0024	.0019	.0015	.0010	.0006	.0001
29	.4243	.3207	.2429	.1846	.1406	.1073	.0630	.0374	.0224	.0135	.0082	.0051	.0031	.0020	.0015	.0012	.0008	.0005	.0001
30	.4120	.3083	.2314	.1741	.1314	.0994	.0573	.0334	.0196	.0116	.0070	.0042	.0026	.0016	.0012	.0010	.0006	.0004	.0000
40	.3066	.2083	.1420	.0972	.0668	.0460	.0221	.0107	.0053	.0026	.0013	.0007	.0004	.0002	.0001	.0001	.0001	.0000	.0000

Table 4: Present Value of an Annuity of $1 = T4(i,n)

Periods	3%	4%	5%	6%	7%	8%	10%	12%	14%	16%	18%	20%	22%	24%
1	.9709	.9615	.9524	.9434	.9346	.9259	.9091	.8929	.8772	.8621	.8475	.8333	.8197	.8065
2	1.9135	1.8861	1.8594	1.8334	1.8080	1.7833	1.7355	1.6901	1.6467	1.6052	1.5656	1.5278	1.4915	1.4568
3	2.8286	2.7751	2.7232	2.6730	2.6243	2.5771	2.4869	2.4018	2.3216	2.2459	2.1743	2.1065	2.0422	1.9813
4	3.7171	3.6299	3.5460	3.4651	3.3872	3.3121	3.1699	3.0373	2.9137	2.7982	2.6901	2.5887	2.4936	2.4043
5	4.5797	4.4518	4.3295	4.2124	4.1002	3.9927	3.7908	3.6048	3.4331	3.2743	3.1272	2.9906	2.8636	2.7454
6	5.4172	5.2421	5.0757	4.9173	4.7665	4.6229	4.3553	4.1114	3.8887	3.6847	3.4976	3.3255	3.1669	3.0205
7	6.2303	6.0021	5.7864	5.5824	5.3893	5.2064	4.8684	4.5638	4.2883	4.0386	3.8115	3.6046	3.4155	3.2423
8	7.0197	6.7327	6.4632	6.2098	5.9713	5.7466	5.3349	4.9676	4.6389	4.3436	4.0776	3.8372	3.6193	3.4212
9	7.7861	7.4353	7.1078	6.8017	6.5152	6.2469	5.7590	5.3282	4.9464	4.6065	4.3030	4.0310	3.7863	3.5655
10	8.5302	8.1109	7.7217	7.3601	7.0236	6.7101	6.1446	5.6502	5.2161	4.8332	4.4941	4.1925	3.9232	3.6819
11	9.2526	8.7605	8.3064	7.8869	7.4987	7.1390	6.4951	5.9377	5.4527	5.0286	4.6560	4.3271	4.0354	3.7757
12	9.9540	9.3851	8.8633	8.3838	7.9427	7.5361	6.8137	6.1944	5.6603	5.1971	4.7932	4.4392	4.1274	3.8514
13	10.6350	9.9856	9.3936	8.8527	8.3577	7.9038	7.1034	6.4235	5.8424	5.3423	4.9095	4.5327	4.2028	3.9124
14	11.2961	10.5631	9.8986	9.2950	8.7455	8.2442	7.3667	6.6282	6.0021	5.4675	5.0081	4.6106	4.2646	3.9616
15	11.9379	11.1184	10.3797	9.7122	9.1079	8.5595	7.6061	6.8109	6.1422	5.5755	5.0916	4.6755	4.3152	4.0013
16	12.5611	11.6523	10.8378	10.1059	9.4466	8.8514	7.8237	6.9740	6.2651	5.6685	5.1624	4.7296	4.3567	4.0333
17	13.1661	12.1657	11.2741	10.4773	9.7632	9.1216	8.0216	7.1196	6.3729	5.7487	5.2223	4.7746	4.3908	4.0591
18	13.7535	12.6593	11.6896	10.8276	10.0591	9.3719	8.2014	7.2497	6.4674	5.8178	5.2732	4.8122	4.4187	4.0799
19	14.3238	13.1339	12.0853	11.1581	10.3356	9.6036	8.3649	7.3658	6.5504	5.8775	5.3162	4.8435	4.4415	4.0967
20	14.8775	13.5903	12.4622	11.4699	10.5940	9.8181	8.5136	7.4694	6.6231	5.9288	5.3527	4.8696	4.4603	4.1103
21	15.4150	14.0292	12.8212	11.7641	10.8355	10.0168	8.6487	7.5620	6.6870	5.9731	5.3837	4.8913	4.4756	4.1212
22	15.9369	14.4511	13.1630	12.0416	11.0612	10.2007	8.7715	7.6446	6.7429	6.0113	5.4099	4.9094	4.4882	4.1300
23	16.4436	14.8568	13.4886	12.3034	11.2722	10.3711	8.8832	7.7184	6.7921	6.0442	5.4321	4.9245	4.4985	4.1371
24	16.9355	15.2470	13.7986	12.5504	11.4693	10.5288	8.9847	7.7843	6.8351	6.0726	5.4509	4.9371	4.5070	4.1428
25	17.4131	15.6221	14.0939	12.7834	11.6536	10.6748	9.0770	7.8431	6.8729	6.0971	5.4669	4.9476	4.5139	4.1474
26	17.8768	15.9828	14.3752	13.0032	11.8258	10.8100	9.1609	7.8957	6.9061	6.1182	5.4804	4.9563	4.5196	4.1511
27	18.3270	16.3296	14.6430	13.2105	11.9867	10.9352	9.2372	7.9426	6.9352	6.1364	5.4919	4.9636	4.5243	4.1542
28	18.7641	16.6631	14.8981	13.4062	12.1371	11.0511	9.3066	7.9844	6.9607	6.1520	5.5016	4.9697	4.5281	4.1566
29	19.1885	16.9837	15.1411	13.5907	12.2777	11.1584	9.3696	8.0218	6.9830	6.1656	5.5098	4.9747	4.5312	4.1585
30	19.6004	17.2920	15.3725	13.7648	12.4090	11.2578	9.4269	8.0552	7.0027	6.1772	5.5168	4.9789	4.5338	4.1601
40	23.1148	19.7928	17.1591	15.0463	13.3317	11.9246	9.7791	8.2438	7.1050	6.2335	5.5482	4.9966	4.5439	4.1659

Table 5: Modified Accelerated Cost Recovery System Classification of Assets Property class

Year	3-year	5-year	7-year	10-year	15-year	20-year
1	33.3%	20.0%	14.3%	10.0%	5.0%	3.8%
2	44.5	32.0	24.5	18.0	9.5	7.2
3	14.8 a	19.2	17.5	14.4	8.6	6.7
4	7.4	11.5 a	12.5	11.5	7.7	6.2
5		11.5	8.9 a	9.2	6.9	5.7
6		5.8	8.9	7.4	6.2	5.3
7			8.9	6.6 a	5.9 a	4.9
8			4.5	6.6	5.9	4.5 a
9				6.5	5.9	4.5
10				6.5	5.9	4.5
11				3.3	5.9	4.5
12					5.9	4.5
13					5.9	4.5
14					5.9	4.5
15					5.9	4.5
16					3.0	4.4
17						4.4
18						4.4
19						4.4
20						4.4
21						2.2
Total	100%	100%	100%	100%	100%	100%

a. Denotes the year of changeover to straight-line depreciation.

Table 6: MACRS Tables by Property Class

MACRS PROPERTY CLASS & DEPRECIATION METHOD	USEFUL LIFE (ADR MIDPOINT LIFE) "A"	EXAMPLES OF ASSETS
3-year property 200% declining balance	4 years or less	Most small tools are included; the law specifically excludes autos and light trucks from this property class.
5-year property 200% declining balance	More than 4 years to less than 10 years	Autos and light trucks, computers, typewriters, copiers, duplicating equipment, heavy general- purpose trucks, and research and experimentation equipment are included.
7-year property 200% and declining balance	10 years or more to less than 16 years	Office furniture and fixtures most items of machinery and equipment used in production are included
10-year property 200% declining balance	16 years or more to less than 20 years	Various machinery and equipment, such as that used in petroleum distilling and refining and in the milling of grain, are included.
15-year property 150% declining balance	20 years or more to less than 25 years	Sewage treatment plants, telephone and electrical distribution facilities, and land improvements are included.
20-year property 150% declining balance	25 years or more	Service stations and other real property with an ADR midpoint life of less than 27.5 years are included.
27.5-year property Straight-line	Not applicable	All residential rental property is included
31.5-year property Straight-line	Not applicable	All nonresidential property is included.

"a" The term ADR midpoint life means the "useful life" of an asset in a business sense; the appropriate ADR midpoint lives for assets are designated in the tax Regulations.

What to Know About the Cost of Capital

The cost of capital is defined as the rate of return that is necessary to maintain the market value of the firm (or price of the firm's stock). Project managers must know whether the cost of capital, often called the *minimum required rate of return*, was used either as a discount rate under the NPV method or as a hurdle rate under the IRR method. The cost of capital is computed as a weighted average of the various capital components, which are items on the right-hand side of the balance sheet such as debt, preferred stock, common stock, and retained earnings.

Cost of Debt

The cost of debt is stated on an after-tax basis, since the interest on the debt is tax deductible. However, the cost of preferred stock is the stated annual dividend rate. This rate is not adjusted for income taxes because the preferred dividend, unlike debt interest, is not a deductible expense in computing corporate income taxes.

Example 17

Assume that the Bridgewood Company issues a $1,000, 8 percent, 20-year bond whose net proceeds are $940. The tax rate is 40 percent. Then, the after-tax cost of debt is:

$$8.00\% \ (1-0.4) = 4.8\%$$

Example 18

Suppose that the Bridgewood Company has preferred stock that pays a $12 dividend per share and sells for $100 per share in the market. Then the cost of preferred stock is:

$$\frac{\text{Dividend per share}}{\text{Price per share}} = \frac{\$12}{\$100} = 12\%$$

Cost of Common Stock

The cost of common stock is generally viewed as the rate of return investors require on a firm's common stock. One way to measure the cost of common stock is to use the *Gordon's growth model*. The model is

$$P_0 = \frac{D_1}{r-g}$$

where P_0 = value (or market price) of common stock

D_1 = dividend to be received in 1 year

r = investor's required rate of return

g = rate of growth (assumed to be constant over time)

Solving the model for r results in the following formula for the cost of common stock:

$$r = \frac{D_1}{P_o} + g$$

Example 19

Assume that the market price of the Bridgewood Company's stock is $40. The dividend to be paid at the end of the coming year is $4 per share and is expected to grow at a constant annual rate of 6 percent. Then the cost of this common stock is:

$$\frac{D_1}{P_o} + g = \frac{\$4}{\$40} + 6\% = 16\%$$

Cost of Retained Earnings

The cost of retained earnings is closely related to the cost of existing common stock, since the cost of equity obtained by retained earnings is the same as the rate of return investors require on the firm's common stock.

Measuring the Overall Cost of Capital

The firm's overall cost of capital is the weighted average of the individual capital costs, with the weights being the proportions of each type of capital used.

Σ (Percentage of the total capital structure supplied by each source of capital x cost of capital for each source)

The computation of overall cost of capital is illustrated in the following example.

Example 20

Assume that the capital structure at the latest statement date is indicative of the proportions of financing that the company intends to use over time:

		Cost
Mortgage bonds ($1,000 par)	$20,000,000	4.80% (from Example 17)
Preferred stock ($100 par)	5,000,000	12.00 (from Example 18)
Common stock ($40 par)	20,000,000	16.00 (from Example 19)
Retained earnings	5,000,000	16.00
Total	$50,000,000	

These proportions would be applied to the assumed individual explicit after-tax costs below:

Source	Weights	Cost	Weighted Cost
Debt	40%(a)	4.80%	1.92%(b)
Preferred stock	10	12.00%	1.20
Common stock	40	16.00%	6.40
Retained earnings	10	16.00%	1.60
	100%		11.12%

(a) $20,000,000/$50,000,000 = .40 = 40\%$
(b) $4.80\% \times 40\% = 1.92\%$

Overall cost of capital is 11.12%

By computing a company's cost of capital, we can determine its minimum rate of return, which is used as the discount rate in present value calculations. A company's cost of capital is also an indicator of risk. For example, if your company's cost of financing increases, it is being viewed as more risky by investors and creditors, who are demanding higher return on their investments in the form of higher dividend and interest rates.

Economic Feasibility Study for an IT Project

Determining economic feasibility requires a careful investigation of the costs and benefits of a proposed information system. The basic framework for feasibility analysis is the *capital budgeting* model in which cost savings and other benefits, as well as initial outlay costs, operating costs, and other cash outflows, are translated into dollar estimates.

The estimated benefits are compared with the costs to determine whether the system is cost beneficial. Where possible, benefits and costs that are not easily quantifiable should be estimated and included in the feasibility analysis. If they cannot be accurately estimated, they should be listed and the likelihood of their occurring and the expected impact on the organization evaluated. Some of the tangible and intangible benefits a company might obtain from a new system are cost savings: improved customer service, productivity, decision making, and data processing: better management control; and increased job satisfaction and employee morale.

Equipment costs are an initial outlay cost if the system is purchased and an operating cost if rented or leased. Equipment costs vary from a few thousands for microcomputer systems to millions of dollars for enormous mainframes. Equipment costs are usually less than the cost of acquiring software and maintaining, supporting, and operating the system. Software acquisition costs include the purchase price of software as well as the time and effort required to design, program, test, and document software. The personnel costs associated with hiring, training, and relocating staff can be substantial. Site preparation costs may be incurred for large computer systems. There are costs involved in installing the new system and converting files to the appropriate format and storage media.

The primary operating cost is maintaining the system. There may be significant annual cash outflows for equipment replacement and expansion and software updates. Human resource costs include the salaries of systems analysts, programmers, operators, data entry operators, and management. Costs are also incurred for supplies, overhead, and other operating costs. Initial cash outlay and operating costs are summarized in Exhibit 29.

Exhibit 30: Initial Cash Outlay and Operating Costs

Hardware

Central processing unit

Peripherals

Special input/output devices

Communications hardware

Upgrade and expansion costs

Software

Application, system, general-purpose, utility, and communications software

Updated versions of software

Application software design, programming, modification, and testing

Installation

Freight and delivery charges

Setup and connection fees

Conversion

Systems testing

File and data conversions

Parallel operations

Documentation

Systems documentation

Training program documentation

Operating standards and procedures

Site preparation

Air-conditioning, humidity, and dust controls

Physical security (access)

Fire and water protection

Cabling, wiring, and outlets

Furnishing and fixtures

Staff

Supervisors

Analysts and programmers

Computer operators

Input (data conversion) personnel

Recruitment and staff training

Maintenance/backup

Hardware/software maintenance

Backup and recovery operations

Power supply protection

Supplies and overhead

Preprinted forms

Data storage devices

Supplies (paper, ribbons, toner)

Utilities and power

Others

Legal and consulting fees

Insurance

During systems design, several alternative approaches to meeting system requirements are developed. Various feasibility measures such as technical, operational, legal, and scheduling feasibility are then used to narrow the list of alternatives. Economic feasibility and capital budgeting techniques, which were discussed earlier, are used to evaluate the benefit-cost aspects of the alternatives.

Example 22

Sophie, an information systems (IS) project manager for the MYK chain of discount stores, is contemplating installation of a new IS system that is flexible, efficient, timely, and responsive to user and customer needs. The new system aims at improving the company's business processes. After the analysis Sophie's IS project team decided they wanted the corporate office to gather daily sales data from each store. Analyzing the prior day's sales will help the company adapt quickly to customer needs. Providing sales data to suppliers will help avoid stockouts and overstocking.

Coordinating buying at the corporate office will help MYK to minimize inventory levels and negotiate lower wholesale prices. Stores will send orders electronically the day they are prepared. Based on store orders, the previous day's sales exhibits, and the warehouse inventory, MYK will send purchase orders to suppliers. Suppliers will process orders and ship goods to regional warehouses or directly to the stores the day orders are received. Each store will have the flexibility to respond to local sales trends and conditions by placing local orders. Accounts payable will be centralized so the firm can make payments electronically.

Sophie's team conducted an economic feasibility study and determined that the project makes excellent use of funds. As shown in Table 9, they estimated that initial outlay costs for the system are $4.32 million (initial systems design and new hardware $1.8 million each, software $375,000, and training, site preparation, and conversion $250,000 each).

The team estimated what it would cost to operate the system for its estimated six-year life, as well as how much the system would save the company. The following recurring costs were identified: hardware expansion, additional software and software updates, systems maintenance, added personnel to operate the system, communication charges, and overhead. The system will also save the company money by eliminating clerical jobs, generating working capital savings, increasing sales and profits, and decreasing warehouse costs. The costs and savings for years 1 through 6, which are expected to rise from year to year, are shown in Table 9.

Sophie calculated the annual savings minus the recurring additional costs and then calculated the annual after-tax cash savings under the MACRS tax rule. The $4.66 million system can be depreciated over the six-year period. For example, the depreciation in year 1 of $932,000 reduces net income by that amount. Since the company does not have to pay taxes on the $1 million, at their tax rate of 34% they end up saving an additional $316,880 in year 1. Finally, Sophie calculated the net savings for each year.

Sophie used MYK's cost of capital of 10% to calculate the net present value (NPV) of the investment, which is over $3 million. The internal rate of return (IRR) is a respectable 26%. Sophie realized how advantageous it would, be for the company' to borrow the money (at 10% interest rates) in order to produce a 26% return on that borrowed money. In addition, payback (the point at which the initial cost is recovered) occurs in the fourth year. NPV and 1RR are calculated as shown in Exhibit 30.

Sophie presented the system and its cost-benefit calculations to top management. Challenges to her estimates (various "what-if" scenarios) were plugged into the Excel model so that management could see the effect of the changed assumptions. This spreadsheet analysis was intended to ensure a positive return of the new system under future uncertainty.

Exhibit 30: Economic Feasibility Study for a New Information System

	Initial Outlay 0	1	2	Years 3	4	5	6
Initial outlay costs (I)							
Initial system design	$ 1,800,000						
Hardware	1,800,000						
Software	375,000						
Training	185,000						
Site preparation	250,000						
Conversion	250,000						
Total	$ 4,660,000						
Recurring costs							
Hardware expansion		$ 70,000	$ 250,000	$ 290,000	$ 330,000	$ 370,000	$ 390,000
Software			120,000	130,000	140,000	150,000	160,000
Systems maintenance			160,000	210,000	230,000	245,000	260,000
Personnel costs		485,000	800,000	900,000	1,000,000	1,100,000	1,300,000
Communication charges		99,000	160,000	180,000	200,000	220,000	250,000
Overhead		310,000	420,000	490,000	560,000	600,000	640,000
Total		$ 964,000	$ 1,910,000	$ 2,200,000	$ 2,460,000	$ 2,685,000	$ 3,000,000
Cash savings							
Clerical cost savings		$ 500,000	$ 1,110,000	$ 1,350,000	$ 1,500,000	$ 1,700,000	$ 1,950,000
Working capital savings		1,000,000	1,200,000	1,500,000	1,500,000	1,500,000	1,500,000
Increased sales and profits			500,000	900,000	1,200,000	1,500,000	1,800,000
Reduced warehouse costs			400,000	800,000	1,200,000	1,600,000	2,000,000
Total		$ 1,500,000	$ 3,210,000	$ 4,550,000	$ 5,400,000	$ 6,300,000	$ 7,250,000
Cash savings minus recurring costs		536,000	1,300,000	2,350,000	2,940,000	3,615,000	4,250,000
Less income taxes (34%) 34%		(182,240)	(442,000)	(799,000)	(999,600)	(1,229,100)	(1,445,000)
Cash savings (net of tax)		$ 353,760	$ 858,000	$ 1,551,000	$ 1,940,400	$ 2,385,900	$ 2,805,000
Tax shield from depreciation		316,880	507,008	304,205	182,206	182,206	91,895
Net cash inflows (net savings) after taxes	$ (4,660,000)	$ 670,640	$ 1,365,008	$ 1,855,205	$ 2,122,606	$ 2,568,106	$ 2,896,895

Tax savings from depreciation deduction

Year	MACRS	Depreciation	Tax savings
1	20.00%	$ 932,000	$ 316,880
2	32.00%	1,491,200	507,008
3	19.20%	894,720	304,205
4	11.50%	535,900	182,206
5	11.50%	535,900	182,206
6	5.80%	270,280	91,895

Net present value calculations @ a cost of capital of 10%

Year	Net savings	PV factor	PV
0	$ (4,660,000)	1.0000	$ (4,660,000)
1	670,640	0.9091	609,679
2	1,365,008	0.8265	1,128,179
3	1,855,205	0.7513	1,393,815
4	2,122,606	0.6830	1,449,740
5	2,568,106	0.6209	1,594,537
6	2,896,895	0.5645	1,635,297
		NPV	$ 3,151,248
		IRR	26.26%

CHAPTER 10

Managing Project Risks

In 2009 the Standish group, a research company that produces annual reports on information technology (IT) projects carried out in the US, reported that only 29 percent of these projects were considered a success, with the vast majority running over time and over budget. Cost overruns averaged 56 percent of original budgets, and projects took on average 84 per cent longer than originally anticipated.

Recent years have been marked by a rapid growth in the use of project management as a means by which industrial, commercial and governmental organizations achieve their objectives. Membership in various international project management associations is growing exponentially, postgraduate programs in project management are appearing everywhere and Microsoft recently claimed to have over 5 million users of its project management software worldwide. This growing maturity of project management, however, does not seem to be reflected in a growing success rate. Ensuring project success – delivering a project on time, within budget and to the client's satisfaction – still seems to be notoriously difficult. The cause for all these failures lies in the fact that projects, especially large-scale ones, are inherently risky ventures. How you deal with those risks will be a major factor in whether your project will succeed or fail.

Project risks can never be fully eliminated, but efforts can be made to reduce the likelihood of risks materializing or mitigating their impact. The goal of project risk management is to identify the main risks, assess their severity and manage them.

The first stage, *risk identification*, is the responsibility of everyone participating in a project, from senior management to team members, client representatives and stakeholders. By identifying risks, you remove the element of surprise, making dealing with the consequences more effective and efficient. Useful tools for risk identification include brainstorming sessions, industry checklists, post-mortem reports of previous projects and a careful analysis of all the assumptions in the project plan. The result is a risk register, which contains a detailed description of all identified risks.

In the *risk assessment* phase, the identified risks are classified according to their likelihood of occurrence and impact, should they materialize. In most projects, risks are so numerous that they cannot all be addressed with the same rigor. The purpose of an assessment is to prioritize them. A framework called a likelihood-impact matrix provides a guideline for focusing your efforts, by distinguishing between extreme, high, medium and low risks. The result is a prioritized risk register. Such a risk assessment needs to be carried out for the three principal dimensions of project risk: scope (quality), time and resources (budget).

In the *risk management* phase, action is taken to prevent or mitigate risks. These actions can include contingency plans, risk avoidance ideas, risk mitigation measures, risk transference, or risk acceptance.

Contingency plans do not tackle a risk directly, but provide ready-to-implement plans to mitigate risks in case they occur. This is a useful exercise, since a generally accepted rule-of-thumb says that developing a solution for an issue once it occurs is ten times more expensive than developing a contingency plan beforehand.

Risk avoidance implies taking a different route altogether that does not have the same level of risk.

Risk mitigation measures can either reduce the likelihood of a risk materializing, or minimize the impact of a risk if it occurs. An example of the former is prototyping, where major issues can be identified while developing a scaled-down version of the project, while an example of the latter is a back-up system that kicks in if the main system malfunctions or is not yet operational.

To illustrate, when a new airport was being built in Denver, Colorado, technical problems repeatedly pushed back its opening date, resulting in a 16-month delay and a cost overrun of more than $2 billion, almost bankrupting the city. The delays were mainly caused by a malfunctioning baggage handling system. A back-up system, costing around $10 million, could have prevented these delays. Unfortunately, the city only decided to implement a back-up system six months after the planned opening date.

The likelihood-impact matrix can also help in understanding how the various risks should be tackled. Risks identified in the top-right quadrant are highly likely events with a major impact, which means they should be incorporated into your plan from the start. The risk of failure for the highly advanced baggage system at Denver Airport was probably in this quadrant, requiring action from the outset. Risks in the bottom-right quadrant require contingency plans. Examples can be found in the Heathrow Terminal 5 project, where plans are in place in the case of terrorist attacks. Risks in the top-left quadrant, of which there will be many, should not be tackled individually, but can be grouped with an overall protection against their joint impact. A typical example is the multitude of minor delays and cost overruns in a project that, when combined, can dramatically affect the project completion but can be tackled by adding time buffers and contingency budgets. Risks in the bottom-left quadrant should not be tackled straightaway, but should be monitored.

The final deliverable of this risk analysis process is a prioritized risk register with assigned responsibilities and action plans.

Timeline Risks

Of the three main project objectives -- scope, time and cost -- time is receiving more and more attention as time-based competition forces companies to launch products and services earlier and at more regular intervals. This makes managing timeline risks a crucial factor in ensuring project success. Every sensible project manager knows that projects are never executed exactly as planned and that delays are inevitable. So the question is how to manage those delays and how to recuperate from them.

Using the framework described above, the first step is to assess the potential impact of delays. To accomplish this, a best-case and worst-case duration estimate for each activity should be determined, along with their expected durations. This enables a calculation of the worst-case outcome to be made, where each activity takes the longest possible time. With this in hand, a rough idea of the potential scale of the problem can be obtained.

However, although things will go wrong in a project, it is unlikely that *everything* will go wrong. Therefore, the second step, a likelihood assessment, is required. For each activity, the likelihood of each of its possible durations should be estimated. This can then be expressed as a distribution, with the duration of an activity specified as anything between its best-case and worst-case estimates, but with more likelihood around the most likely duration.

A simulation analysis can then be performed, examining hundreds or thousands of different scenarios, in which the durations of the activities are varied according to their distribution. Software tools such as *@Risk for Project*, which links into *Microsoft Project*, can be used for this analysis. The result is a range for the overall project duration, with likelihood estimates of being able to complete the project by a certain date.

A simulation also reveals which activities are largely responsible for the potential delays. Traditional project planning results in the identification of a critical path, a sequence of activities from the project start to the project finish that determines the project completion date, with delays in any of those critical activities resulting in a delay of the project. Although the concept of criticality is extremely useful and allows the project manager to focus on a limited set of activities in a project instead of scattering his focus, unexpected events may change the activities to be identified as critical. This means that major delays could arise if the project manager continues to focus on those activities initially identified as critical, but subsequently moved from that list.

Using a simulation analysis, one can check which activities in the examined scenarios are responsible for project delays. Some activities will be critical in every examined scenario, and others will never be critical. However, some will be critical only in some scenarios. These activities also require close monitoring, because although they may not be critical at the outset, they can become so because of unexpected delays. A simulation analysis provides a so-called Criticality Index, which is the likelihood that an activity will become critical, based on the number of scenarios in which it was observed to be critical. The criticality indices can then be used to prioritize attention when monitoring activities for possible delays.

A simulation analysis can also reveal which activities contribute most to delays, both in terms of whether or not they have an impact, but also how big the impact is. The latter is not captured by the criticality index, and depends on the risk inherent to each activity. Activities that score highly in this respect are sometimes called crucial activities, to distinguish them from critical ones.

Buffer Management

Besides adding a time contingency or buffer at the end of the project between the expected completion date and the deadline, time buffers can also be inserted at specific points in a project's schedule to prevent an unexpected delay in an activity impacting project delivery. Such buffers should be inserted whenever critical tasks require non-critical work to be completed first. In that case, one should ensure that there is some safety time between the non-critical task and the critical task depending on it. These so-called feeding buffers prevent delays in non-critical paths of the project spreading to the critical path.

Budget Risks

Budget risks can be analyzed in a similar way to timeline risks, with three estimates given for each activity: a pessimistic, optimistic, and likely cost estimate. A simulation analysis will then reveal the expected cost and contingency required so that the budget should be sufficient to cope with unexpected cash outlays. A tornado diagram will also highlight those activities that are responsible for the major budget risks.

Portfolio Risk

Risks embedded in projects contribute to the overall risk profile of the organization in which the projects are carried out. Therefore, project risk management should not only be performed for each project individually, but also for the organization's overall portfolio.

Project portfolio risk management is concerned with making decisions on which projects to pursue, which to initiate and which to terminate, based on a financial and strategic assessment of the expected benefits and associated risks. Such an analysis is typically based on a net present value analysis, enhanced with sensitivity analysis, scenario analysis and simulation analysis in which the impact of the technical and commercial risks is assessed. Based on the risk appetite of the organization, a specific portfolio of projects is proposed.

Consider for instance the pharmaceutical industry. Drug discovery and development is an extremely risky, time-consuming and expensive process. The average time from compound to market has grown to more than 12 years, with recent estimates indicating that the cost of developing a medicine is around $1 billion.

The main issue, however, is the low chance of a drug in development actually reaching the market. The vast majority of drugs in development do not make it through the stringent scientific and regulatory procedures required and are terminated. And of the drugs that do reach the market, only 30 percent achieve the commercial success necessary to recover the development costs to yield a healthy return.

Large pharmaceutical companies such as Pfizer, GlaxoSmithKline and Novartis are highly advanced in their portfolio risk management processes, which are believed to be a core success factor in establishing and maintaining profitability. Recently, smaller biotech companies have also embraced risk management, considerably reducing the huge risk that is typically associated with these ventures.

Risk Analysis Tools for Project Management

Risk analysis is important in making project management decisions because of the large amount of capital involved and the long-term nature of the investments being considered. The higher the risk associated with a proposed project, the greater the rate of return that must be earned on the project to compensate for that risk.

Since different investment projects involve different risks, it is important to incorporate risk into the analysis of capital budgeting. There are several methods for incorporating risk, including:

1 Probability distributions
2 Risk-adjusted discount rate
3 Certainty equivalent
4 Sensitivity analysis
5 Decision trees (or probability trees)
6 Simulation

Probability Distributions

Expected values of a probability distribution may be computed. Before any capital budgeting method is applied, compute the expected cash inflows, or in some cases, the expected life of the asset.

Example 1

A firm is considering a $30,000 investment in equipment that will generate cash savings from operating costs. The following estimates regarding cash savings and useful life, along with their respective probabilities of occurrence, have been made:

ANNUAL CASH SAVINGS	PROBABILITY	USEFUL LIFE	PROBABILITY
$6,000	0.2	4 years	0.2
$8,000	0.5	5 years	0.6
$10,000	0.3	6 years	0.2

Then, the expected annual saving is:

$6,000 (0.2)	=	$1,200
$8,000 (0.5)	=	4,000
$10,000 (0.3)	=	3,000
		$8,200

The expected useful life is:

4 (0.2)	=	0.8
5 (0.6)	=	3.0
6 (0.2)	=	1.2
		5

The expected NPV is computed as follows (assuming a 10 percent cost of capital):

$$NPV = PV-I = \$8,200 \ T4(10\%,5)-\$30,000$$

$$= \$8,200 \ (3.7908)-\$30,000 = \$31,085-\$30,000 = \$1,08\uparrow$$

The expected IRR is computed as follows: By definition, at IRR,

I	=	PV
$30,000	=	$8,200 T4 (r,5)

$$T4(r,5) = \frac{\$30,000}{\$8,200} = 3.6585$$

which is about halfway between 10 percent and 12 percent in Table 2.4 in Chapter 2, so that we can estimate the rate to be about 11 percent. Therefore, the equipment should be purchased, since (1) NPV = $1,085, which is positive, and/or (2) IRR = 11 percent, which is greater than the cost of capital of 10 percent.

Risk-Adjusted Discount Rate

This method of risk analysis adjusts the cost of capital (or discount rate) upward as projects become riskier, i.e., a risk-adjusted discount rate is the riskless rate plus a risk premium. Therefore, by increasing the discount rate from 10 percent to 15 percent, the expected cash flow from the investment must be relatively larger or the increased discount rate will generate a negative NPV, and the proposed acquisition/investment would be turned down. The expected cash flows are discounted at the risk-adjusted discount rate and then the usual capital budgeting criteria such as NPV and IRR are applied.

Note: The use of the risk-adjusted discount rate is based on the assumption that investors demand higher returns for riskier projects.

Example 2

A firm is considering an investment project with an expected life of 3 years. It requires an initial investment of $35,000. The firm estimates the following data in each of the next 4 years:

AFTER-TAX CASH INFLOW	PROBABILITY
-$5,000	0.2
$10,000	0.3
$30,000	0.3
$50,000	0.2

Assuming a risk-adjusted required rate of return (after taxes) of 20 percent is appropriate for the investment projects of this level or risk, compute the risk-adjusted NPV. First, the present value is:

PV = -$5,000(0.2) + $10,000(0.3) + $30,000(0.3) + $50,000(0.2)=$21,000

The expected NPV = $21,000 T4(20%,3) - $35,000

= 21,000 (2.107)-$35,000 = $44,247 - $35,000 = $9,247

Certainty Equivalent Approach

The certainty equivalent approach to risk analysis is to convert cash flows from individual projects into risk adjusted certainty equivalent cash flows. The approach is drawn directly from the concept of utility theory. This method forces the decision maker to specify at what point the firm is indifferent to the choice between a certain sum of money and the expected value of a risky sum.

Under this approach, first determine a *certainty equivalent adjustment factor*, a, as:

$$a = \frac{\text{Certain sum}}{\text{Equivalent risky sum}}$$

Once a's are obtained, they are multiplied by the original cash flow to obtain the equivalent certain cash flow. Then, the accept-or-reject decision is made, using the normal capital budgeting criteria. The risk-free rate of return is used as the discount rate under the NPV method and as the cutoff rate under the IRR method. The risk-free rate is the return on a risk-free investment such as Treasury bills. Certainty equivalent adjustments involve a technique directly drawn from utility theory. It forces the decision maker to specify at what point the firm is indifferent to the choice between a sum of money that is certain and the expected value of a risky sum.

Example 3

XYZ, Inc., with a 14 percent cost of capital after taxes is considering a project with an expected life of 4 years. The project requires an initial certain cash outlay of $50,000. The expected cash inflows and certainty equivalent coefficients are as follows:

YEAR	AFTER-TAX CASH FLOW	CERTAINTY EQUIVALENT ADJUSTMENT FACTOR
1	$10,000	0.95
2	15,000	0.80
3	20,000	0.70
4	25,000	0.60

Assuming that the risk-free rate of return is 5 percent, the NPV and IRR are computed as follows:

First, the equivalent certain cash inflows are obtained as follows:

YEAR	AFTER-TAX CASH INFLOW	A	EQUIVALENT CERTAIN CASH INFLOW	PV AT 5%	PV
1	10,000	0.95	$9,500	0.9524	$9,048
2	15,000	0.80	12,000	0.9070	10,884
3	20,000	0.70	14,000	0.8638	12,093
4	25,000	0.60	15,000	0.8227	12,341
					44,366

NPV = $44,366 - $50,000 = -$5,634

By trial and error, we obtain 4 percent as the IRR. Therefore, the project should be rejected, since (1) NPV = -$5,634, which is negative and/or (2) IRR = 4 percent is less than the risk-free rate of 5 percent.

Sensitivity Analysis

Forecasts of many calculated NPVs under various alternative functions are compared to see how sensitive NPV is to changing conditions. It may be found that a certain variable or group of variables, once their assumptions are changed or relaxed, drastically alters the NPV. This results in a much riskier asset than was originally forecast.

Decision Trees

Some firms use decision trees (probability trees) to evaluate the risk of capital budgeting proposals. A decision tree is a graphical method of showing the sequence of possible outcomes. A capital budgeting tree would show the cash flows and NPV of the project under different possible circumstances. The decision tree method has the following advantages: (1) It visually lays out all the possible outcomes of the proposed project and makes management aware of the adverse possibilities, and (2) the conditional nature of successive years' cash flows can be expressly depicted. The disadvantages are: (1) most problems are too complex to permit year-by-year depiction and (2) it does not recognize risk.

Example 4

Assume XYZ Corporation wishes to introduce one of two products to the market this year. The probabilities and present values (PV) of projected cash inflows are given below:

PRODUCT	INITIAL INVESTMENT	PV OF CASH INFLOWS	PROBABILITIES
A	$225,000		1.00
		$450,000	0.40
		200,000	0.50
		-100,000	0.10
B	80,000		1.00
		320,000	0.20
		100,000	0.60
		-150,000	0.20

A decision tree analyzing the two products is given in Exhibit 31.

Exhibit 31: Decision Tree

DECISION TREE

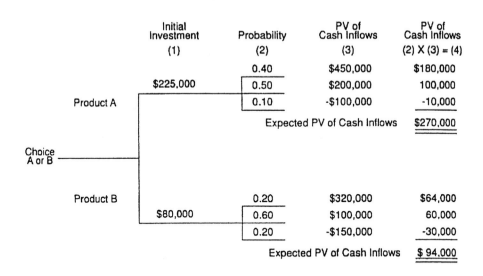

Expected net present value:

Product A	$270,000 - $225,000	=	$45,000
Product B	$ 94,000 - $ 80,000	=	$14,000

Based on the expected NPV, choose product A over product B.

Simulation

This risk analysis method is frequently called Monte Carlo simulation. This technique involves using random numbers and probability to solve problems. The term Monte Carlo Method was coined by S. Ulam and Nicholas Metropolis in reference to games of chance, a popular attraction in Monte Carlo, Monaco. Monte Carlo simulation requires that a probability distribution be constructed for each of the important variables affecting the project's cash flows. Since a computer is used to generate many results using random numbers, project simulation is expensive.

Using Software to Assist in Project Risk Management

Software tools can be used to enhance various risk management processes. Databases can keep track of risks, spreadsheets can aid in tracking and quantifying risks, and more sophisticated risk management software can help you develop models and use simulations to analyze and respond to various risks.

You can use *Microsoft Project* to perform PERT analysis. You can also use add-on software to *Project* to perform Monte Carlo simulations. For example, *Deltek Risk+* (www.deltek.com/products/riskplus/) is a comprehensive risk analysis tool that integrates with *Microsoft® Project* to quantify the cost and schedule uncertainty associated with project plans. Predicting how long a project will take or how much it will cost is almost impossible and single point estimates for task duration and cost can be misleading. Risk+ brings these capabilities to Microsoft Project. The combination of Risk+ and Microsoft Project provides an extremely powerful project management toolset that is both affordable and easy to use. It uses Monte Carlo-based simulation techniques to answer questions such as: What are the chances of completing the project by December 1, 2012? How confident are we that costs will remain below $10 million? What are the chances that this task will end up on the critical path?

To use a Monte Carlo simulation to estimate the probability of meeting specific schedule goals, you would collect optimistic, pessimistic, and most likely duration estimates for project tasks on a project network diagram, similar to the PERT technique. However, you must also collect estimates for the probability of completing each task between the optimistic and most likely times. The same approach can be used for cost estimates. You would collect optimistic, pessimist, and most likely estimates for factors that determine project costs and the probability of the cost factors being between the optimistic and most likely values. For example, an expert might estimate that a certain task will most likely take three months to complete, but it could take as little as one month or up to nine months. When asked the probability of completing the task between one and three months, the expert might honestly reply that the probability is only 20 percent. Another expert might estimate that another project task will take five months to complete, but it could take as little as two months or it could take up to seven months. This expert might estimate that the probability of completing that task between two and five months was 80 percent. Estimating the probability of completing tasks between the optimistic and most likely times helps to account for estimating bias. Compared with a PERT calculation, the Monte Carlo approach simulates various probability distributions for each estimate instead of applying the same simple PERT variation for all estimated durations.

You can use Monte Carlo simulations to help estimate project costs. First you would develop a model for estimating the total project cost. Suppose project costs could be estimated based on the number of pounds of a certain material, the cost per pound of the material, the number of hours of specific workers, and the cost per hour for each category of worker (such as managers, programmers, electrical engineers, and so on). You could run a Monte Carlo simulation of the total project cost based on estimates of the optimistic, pessimistic, and most likely number of pounds of material, costs per pound of the material, number of hours of specific workers, and the cost per hour for the various workers.

Exhibit 32 shows the results of a Monte Carlo simulation to estimate total project cost. These simulation results show that there is a 20 percent chance of the project costing less than $175,693, a 65 percent chance of it costing less than $180,015, and a 95 percent chance of the total project cost being under $184,528. For example, you can use this information to decide how much to bid on a project, if you are the seller, or how much to budget for the project, if you are the buyer, based on your risk tolerance. For example, if you are risk-averse, you might want to bid $185,000 to be extremely confident that you will not go over budget.

Exhibit 32: Sample Monte Carlo Simulation Results for Project Cost

Number of Samples: 250
Unique ID: 1
Name: Widget

Cost Std Deviation: $3,290
95% Confidence Interval: $408
Each bar represents $1,000

Completion Probability Table

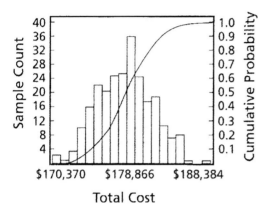

$170,370 $178,866 $188,384

Total Cost

Prob	Cost	Prob	Cost
0.05	$173,748	0.55	$179,327
0.10	$174,472	0.60	$179,556
0.15	$175,266	0.65	$180,015
0.20	$175,693	0.70	$180,518
0.25	$176,362	0.75	$180,984
0.30	$176,940	0.80	$181,611
0.35	$177,597	0.85	$182,387
0.40	$177,963	0.90	$183,208
0.45	$178,508	0.95	$184,528
0.50	$178,973	1.00	$188,384

In addition to estimating overall probabilities of project goals such as completion dates or cost estimates, top sources of risk (risk drivers) can also be found. For example, a cost simulation might show that the number of labor hours for the electrical engineers was the main source of cost risk for a project.

Simulations are a very powerful tool, and it is important that people who use them understand all of the variables, inputs, and outputs involved. As with any software product, the information that comes out is only as good as the information that goes in. It is important to collect data from people who understand the project or specific tasks involved. It is also important to test the model used in simulations to ensure it provides realistic results.

Good project risk management often goes unnoticed, unlike crisis management With crisis management, there is an obvious danger to the success of a project. The crisis, in turn, receives the intense interest of the entire project team.

Resolving a crisis has much greater visibility, often accompanied by rewards from management, than successful risk management. In contrast, when risk management is effective, it results in fewer problems, and for the few problems that exist, it results in more expeditious resolutions. It may be difficult for outside observers to tell whether risk management or luck was responsible for the smooth development of a new system, but teams will always know that their projects worked out better because of good risk management.

CHAPTER 11

Project Communication and Documentation

This chapter discusses an element vital to the effective performance of a project—communication. Communication takes place between the project team and the customer, among the project team members, and between the project team and its upper management. Communication may involve two people or a group of people. It can be oral or written. It can be face to face or involve some medium, such as phone, voice mail, electronic mail, letters, memos, video conferencing, or groupware. It can be formal, such as a report or a presentation at a meeting, or informal, such as a hallway conversation or an email message. This chapter covers many communication formats.

Personal Communication

Effective and frequent personal communication is crucial to keeping the project moving, identifying potential problems, soliciting suggestions for improving project performance, keeping abreast of whether the customer is satisfied, and avoiding surprises. Personal communication can occur through words or nonverbal behavior, such as body language. It can be face to face or use some medium, including telephone, voice mail, electronic mail, letters, memos, video conferencing, or groupware. Personal communication can be oral or written.

Oral Communication

Personal oral communication can be face to face or via telephone. It can be by means of voice mail or video conferencing. Information can be communicated in a more accurate and timely manner orally. Such communication provides a forum for discussion, clarification, understanding, and immediate feedback. Face-to-face communication also provides an opportunity to observe the body language that accompanies the communication. Even phone conversations allow the listener to hear the tone, inflection, and emotion of the voice. Body language and tone are important elements that enrich oral communication. Face-to-face situations provide an even greater opportunity for enriched communication than phone conversations do.

Body language can be used not only by the person talking, but also by the listener, as a way of providing feedback to the person talking. Positive body language can include direct eye contact, a smile, hand gestures, forward leaning, and nodding acknowledgment or agreement. Negative body language can be a frown, crossed arms, slouching, fidgeting, gazing or looking away, doodling, or yawning. In personal communications *people need to be sensitive to body language reflective of the cultural diversity of the participants,* whether they're other team members or the customer. When communicating with individuals from other cultures or countries, you need to be aware of their customs regarding greetings, gestures, gift giving, and protocol. For example, hand gestures, proximity to the person with whom you are communicating, and touching have different meanings in different cultures.

When communicating orally, a person must be careful not to use remarks, words, or phrases that can be construed as sexist, racist, prejudicial, or offensive. Comments do not have to be made directly to a particular person to be offensive. Remarks made in a group setting can be distasteful to some individuals in the group. They may find certain statements hurtful to themselves or to an acquaintance. Comments about ethnic customs, surnames, dialects, religious practices, physical characteristics or appearance, or mannerisms can be offensive, even if the offense is unintentional or the comment is said in jest.

A high degree of face-to-face communication is especially important early in a project to foster team building, develop good working relationships, allow for immediate feedback, and establish mutual expectations. Locating the project team in a common area facilitates communication. It's much easier to walk over to someone's office to ask something than to call the person on the phone and maybe wait several days for your call to be returned. However, voice mail allows individuals to communicate orally in a timely manner when face-to-face communication is not possible. It is not always feasible to locate the project team in a common area, especially if the team includes members or subcontractors from different geographic locations. In such cases, video conferencing can be helpful, if available.

Project team members need to be proactive in initiating timely communication with other team members and the project manager, rather than waiting until an upcoming project team meeting that could be several weeks away. The project manager, in particular, should get out of the office on a regular basis and drop in on individual team members. He or she should take the initiative to visit the customer or the firm's upper management for face-to-face communication, rather than waiting to be summoned to a meeting. If a visit to the customer requires distant travel, the manager should initiate regular phone discussions between visits.

Oral communication should be straightforward and unambiguous. Sometimes attempting to be overly tactful, especially in communicating a problem or concern, can mislead and result in unclear expectations. You should check for understanding of what you wanted to communicate by asking for feedback. If you're not sure whether a point you made was understood by the other person, ask the other person to state his or her understanding of what you said. Similarly, if you aren't clear on a point the other person was trying to communicate, paraphrase what you think the other person said to ensure mutual understanding.

Finally, the timing of oral communication is important. For example, you shouldn't barge into a colleague's office and interrupt him if he is in the middle of doing something important. Rather, in such a situation, ask him when would be a good time to get together. You should indicate about how long you need to talk with him and what you want to discuss. He will then know whether to expect a ten-minute discussion on a trivial subject or a one-hour discussion on a critical subject. Similarly, when making a phone call to another person, you should state at the start what topics you want to discuss and how long **it** might take, then ask if now is a good time or if you should call back at a more convenient time.

Written Communication

Personal written communication is generally carried out through internal memos to the project team and external letters to the customer or others outside the firm, such as subcontractors. Memos and letters can be transmitted in hardcopy or through electronic mail (email) or groupware.

Memos and letters are ways to communicate efficiently with a group of people when it's impractical to have a meeting or when the information needs to be disseminated in a timely manner. Written communication should be used only when necessary and not just to generate paperwork. Project participants are usually very busy and do not have time to read trivial memos containing information that could have been communicated orally at the next project meeting.

A memo or letter may be appropriate as a follow-up to a face-to-face conversation or a phone call, so as to confirm decisions or actions rather than relying on a person's memory. When a memo is used to confirm oral communication, other people who were not involved in the oral communication but who may need to know the information can be given copies. Also, such written communication can be important if a member of the project team leaves the project—the replacement person will have a record of communications regarding previous actions and decisions.

Written communication should be used mostly to inform, confirm, and request—for example, to remind the project team that the customer will be visiting on a certain date or to ask team members to provide written input for a quarterly project progress report to the client.

Memos and letters should be clear and concise and should not include lengthy dissertations or voluminous extraneous attachments. Project participants are busy with their assigned work tasks and will perceive being flooded with paperwork or email as more of a hindrance than a help.

Meetings

A meeting can be a vehicle for fostering team building and reinforcing team members' expectations, roles, and commitment to the project objective. This section covers various types of meetings that may take place during a project and provides suggestions for ensuring that meetings are effective.

Types of Project Meetings

The three most common types of project meetings are
- ▶ Status review meetings
- ▶ Problem-solving meetings
- ▶ Technical design review meetings

It's not unusual for a contract between a customer and a project contractor to outline requirements for periodic status review meetings and specific technical review meetings.

Status Review Meetings

A project status review meeting is usually led or called by the project manager; it generally involves all or some of the project team, plus the customer and/or the project team's upper management. The primary purposes of such a meeting are to inform, to identify problems, and to identify action items. Project status meetings should be held on a regularly scheduled basis so that problems and potential problems can be identified early and surprises that could jeopardize accomplishing the project objective can be prevented. For example, project status review meetings might be held weekly with the project team and less frequently with the customer—perhaps monthly or quarterly, depending on the overall duration of the project and the contractual requirements.

A sample agenda for a project status review meeting is shown in Exhibit 33.

Exhibit 33: Project Status Review Meeting Agenda

9:00am Accomplishments since last meeting
- Hardware
- Software
- Documentation

9:30　Cost, schedule, and work scope
- Status
- Trends
- Forecasts
- Variances

9:45　Corrective actions, if necessary

10:15　Opportunities for improvement

10:30　Open discussion

10:50　Action item assignments

11:00　Adjourn

Here are some of the subjects that might be discussed under each of the agenda items:

- *Accomplishments since last meeting.* Key project milestones that were reached should be identified, and actions on items from previous meetings should be reviewed.
- *Cost, schedule, and work scope—status.* Performance should be compared to the baseline plan. It's important that status be based on up-to-date information regarding completed tasks and actual expenditures.
- *Cost, schedule, and work scope—trends.* Any positive or negative trends in project performance should be identified. Even if a project is ahead of schedule, the fact that the schedule has been slipping over the past several weeks might indicate that corrective action should be initiated now, before the project falls behind schedule.
- *Cost, schedule, and work scope—forecasts.* Based on current status, trends, and the project tasks yet to be completed, the forecasted project completion date and forecasted cost at completion should be reviewed and compared to the project objective and the baseline plan.

145

▶ *Cost, schedule, and work scope—variances.* Any differences should be identified between actual progress and planned progress with respect to cost and schedule for project work packages and tasks. These variances can be positive—for example, being ahead of schedule—or they can be negative—such as overrunning the budget given the amount of work that has been accomplished. Negative variances will help pinpoint both current problems and potential problems. Particular attention should be given to those parts of the project that have had negative variances which are continuing to get worse.

▶ *Corrective actions.* In some instances, corrective actions to address problems and potential problems might take place right at the status review meeting—for example, receiving customer or management approval to proceed with the purchase of certain materials or authorization of overtime to get the project back on schedule. In other cases, separate problem-solving meetings may be required so that appropriate members of the project team can develop corrective actions.

▶ *Opportunities for improvement.* These should also be identified, along with problem areas and associated corrective actions. For example, a member of the project team might point out that the technical specifications could be met by using an alternative material or piece of equipment, which is substantially less expensive than the one the team originally planned to use. Or a team member might suggest that substantial time could be saved by replicating and slightly modifying existing computer software rather than developing completely new software.

▶ *Action item assignment.* Specific action items should be identified and assigned to specific team members. For each action item, the person responsible and the estimated completion date should be noted. The completion date should be estimated by the person responsible for the action item. When people verbalize their commitment to a date at a meeting in front of other people, they will usually strive to meet that date.

It should be noted that listening to the information provided at a status review meeting is one way, but not the only way, for a project manager to get a true understanding of the project status. He or she needs to validate what was said at the status review meeting through personal communication with individual members of the project team. The project manager should also ask to see any tangible products, or deliverables, such as drawings, prototypes, or reports. This will both validate that the item is really complete (and not just almost or essentially complete) and show that the project manager is genuinely interested in the individual's work and acknowledges its importance to the successful achievement of the project objective.

Problem-Solving Meetings

When a problem or potential problem is identified by an individual project team member, that person should promptly call a problem-solving meeting with other appropriate individuals, not wait for a future status review meeting. Identifying and resolving problems as early as possible is critical to project success.

The project manager and the project team need to establish guidelines at the beginning of the project regarding who should initiate problem-solving meetings and when, as well as the level of authorization required to implement corrective actions.

Problem-solving meetings should follow a good problem-solving approach, such as the following:

1. Develop a problem statement.
2. Identify potential causes of the problem.
3. Gather data and verify the most likely causes.
4. Identify possible solutions.
5. Evaluate the alternative solutions.
6. Determine the best solution.
7. Revise the project plan.
8. Implement the solution.
9. Determine whether the problem has been solved.

Technical Design Review Meetings

Projects that involve a design phase, such as an information system project, may require one or more technical design review meetings to ensure that the customer agrees with or approves of the design approach developed by the project contractor.

Take the example of a company that hires a consultant to design, develop, and implement an information system to track customer orders from order entry through receipt of payment. The company may require that the consultant review the system design with appropriate company representatives before the next phase of the project—detailed development of the system and purchase of hardware and software—is approved. At a later stage in the project, the company may want certain employees to review and approve the computer interface and output formats developed by the consultant to ensure that they meet the needs and expectations of the people who will be using the system.

▶ *Prepare visual aids or handouts*. Graphics, charts, tables, diagrams, pictures, and physical models are effective visual aids. Often these materials focus the discussion and prevent a lot of rambling and misunderstanding. A picture is worth a thousand words.

▶ *Make meeting room arrangements*. The room should be large enough that people aren't cramped and uncomfortable. Seats should be arranged so that all participants can see each other; this will foster participation. The appropriate visual aids and accessories (projector, screen, videotape player, flip charts, chalkboard) should be in the room and be tested before the meeting starts. Refreshments should be ordered if the meeting is going to be long. For example, box lunches may be served in order to allow meeting discussions to continue over a working lunch.

In some cases, a conference room may be designated the "project room," where all project meetings are held or where project team members can meet for problem-solving discussions.

Sometimes such project rooms have project plans, schedules, status charts, and system diagrams posted on the walls for easy reference by all project team members.

In many technical projects there are two design review meetings:

1. *A preliminary design review meeting* when the contractor has completed the initial conceptual specifications, drawings, or flowcharts. The purpose of this preliminary design review meeting is to get the customer's agreement that the design approach meets the technical requirements and to gain approval from the customer before the contractor orders materials that have a long delivery time (so as not to delay the project schedule).

2. *A final design review meeting* when the contractor has completed the detailed specifications, drawings, screen and report formats, and such. The purpose of this final design review meeting is to gain approval from the customer before the contractor starts building, assembling, and producing the project deliverables.

Effective Meetings

Before, during, and after a meeting, the person calling or conducting the meeting can take various steps to ensure that the meeting is effective.

Before the Meeting

▶ *Determine whether a meeting is really necessary* or whether another mechanism, such as a conference call, is more appropriate.

▶ *Determine the purpose of the meeting*. For instance, is it to share information, plan, collect input or ideas, make a decision, persuade or sell, solve a problem, or evaluate status?

▶ *Determine who needs to participate in the meeting*, given its purpose. The number of participants should be the minimum number needed to achieve the purpose of the meeting. Project team members are usually busy on their work tasks and do not want to participate in meetings to which they have nothing to contribute or from which they have nothing to gain. Individuals who are invited to attend the meeting should know why they are being asked to participate.

▶ *Distribute an agenda well in advance of the meeting* to those invited. The agenda should include:
- ✓ Purpose of the meeting
- ✓ Topics to be covered. (Items should be listed from most important to least important. If time runs out, the most important items will have been covered.)
- ✓ Time allocated for each topic and who will cover the topic, make the presentation, or lead the discussion.

Accompanying the agenda should be any documents or data the participants need to review *prior* to the meeting. Sufficient time should be given between distribution of the announcement and the date of the meeting to allow participants to prepare for the meeting adequately. Some participants may need to collect and analyze data or prepare presentation or handout materials.

During the Meeting

▶ *Start the meeting on time.* If the meeting leader waits for a few late— comers, people will get in the habit of showing up late, because they know the meeting won't start on time anyway. If the meeting starts on time, people will get in the habit of arriving on time rather than suffer the embarrassment of entering a meeting al— ready in progress.

▶ *Designate a note-taker.* Someone should be assigned (preferably before the meeting) to take notes. The notes should be concise, and they should cover decisions and action items, assignments, and estimated completion dates. Detailed meeting minutes can be a burden both to take and to read later and therefore should be avoided.

▶ *Review the purpose of the meeting and the agenda.* Be concise, and don't give a lengthy discourse.

▶ *Facilitate—don't dominate--the meeting.* The project manager should not lead all the discussions, but rather should get other participants to lead the discussions on their assigned topics. A good facilitator will
- ✓ Keep the meeting moving and within the scheduled time frame.
- ✓ Encourage participation, especially from individuals who appear hesitant to participate.
- ✓ Limit discussion by participants who have a tendency to talk too much, repeat themselves, or stray from the topic at hand.
- ✓ Control interruptions and side conversations.
- ✓ Clarify points that are made.

✓ Summarize discussions and make transitions to the next topics on the agenda.

It's helpful to discuss meeting guidelines at a project team meeting at the beginning of the project so that everyone understands what behavior is expected during project meetings.

▶ *Summarize the meeting results* at the end of the meeting, and make sure all participants have a clear understanding of all decisions and action items. The meeting leader should verbalize these items to help avoid any misunderstandings.

▶ *Do not overrun the scheduled meeting time.* Participants may have other commitments or subsequent meetings. If all agenda items are not covered, it's better to schedule another meeting for the people involved with those items. These should be the lower-priority items anyway, since the agenda topics should have been arranged in order of most to least important.

▶ *Evaluate the meeting process.* Occasionally, at the end of a meeting, the participants should openly discuss what took place and determine whether any changes should be made to improve the effectiveness of future meetings.

After the Meeting

Publish the meeting results within 24 hours after the meeting. The summary document should be concise and kept to one page if possible. It should confirm decisions that were made and list the action items, including who is responsible, the estimated completion date, and expected deliverables. It may also list who attended and who was absent. The meeting results should be distributed to all individuals who were invited, whether or not they actually attended the meeting. The meeting notes should not include a detailed narrative of the meeting discussions. Exhibit 34 is a sample action item list from a meeting. Effective meetings, like successful projects, require good planning and good performance.

Presentations

Often the project manager or members of the project team are called on to give a formal presentation. The audience may be representatives of the customer's organization, the project organization's upper management, the project team itself, or the public, such as at a conference.

The audience may be one person (the customer) or several hundred attendees at a national conference. The presentation may last ten minutes or an hour or more. The subject could be an overview of the project; the current status of the project; a serious problem that is jeopardizing successful achievement of the project objective, such as a forecasted schedule delay or cost overrun; or an attempt to persuade the customer to expand or redirect the project work scope.

In such situations, you, the speaker, are in the spotlight. Following are some suggestions that may help you prepare and deliver your presentation.

Exhibit 34: Action Item List from March 1 Project Status Review Meeting

	ACTION	WHO	BY WHEN
1.	Revise system requirements document	Tyler	June 5
2.	Schedule review meeting with customer	David	June 6
3.	Change purchase order for computers from 15 to 20	Suzy	June 11
4.	Evaluate feasibility of bar coding and optical character recognition for data entry	Mary	June 15

Preparing for the Presentation

▶ *Determine the purpose of the presentation.* Is it to inform or to persuade? What do you want to accomplish? For example, do you want the audience to understand the project, or do you want the customer to agree to suggested changes in the project work scope?

▶ *Know the audience.* What is their level of knowledge or familiarity with the subject? What is their rank—are they senior managers and key decision makers, or are they your peers?

▶ *Make an outline of the presentation.* Only after you have made an outline should you write out the presentation. Read it over and over and over, but don't try to memorize it.

▶ *Use simple language that the audience will understand.* Don't use jargon or acronyms that the audience may not understand. Don't use sophisticated or technical vocabulary that the audience may not understand. Don't try to impress the audience with your word power. Don't make remarks that can be construed to be sexist, racist, prejudicial, offensive, sarcastic, or profane.

▶ *Prepare notes or a final outline that you will use or refer to during your presentation.* Yes, it is all right to use notes.

▶ *Practice, practice, practice-more than you think you should.* You may want to do a trial run in front of your peers. Ask for their feedback; solicit suggestions on how you might improve the presentation.

▶ *Prepare visual aids and test them.* Make sure the visual aids are readable from the most distant seat in the room where the presentation will be given. If it will be given in a large auditorium, make sure the visual aids are very large. Visual aids such as graphs, diagrams, and tables should be simple and not too busy—there shouldn't be a lot of text and diagrams shouldn't be too detailed. There should be one idea per chart or slide. Multicolor graphics are more appealing than plain black and white, but choose colors carefully—you can overwhelm your audience with too many colors or color combinations that are difficult to read.

▶ *Make copies of handout materials*. If audience members don't have to take a lot of notes, they will be able to give their full attention to the presentation.

▶ *Request the audiovisual equipment well in advance*. Whether it's an overhead projector, slide projector, microphone, lectern, pointer, or video projector, you don't want to find at the last minute that it's not available.

▶ *Go into the meeting room when it's empty or not in use and get a feel for the surroundings*. Stand in the place where the presentation will be made (in the front of the room, at the lectern, or on the stage). Test the projector and microphone.

Delivering the Presentation

▶ *Expect a bit of nervousness*; all speakers experience it. Just remember that you know more about what you are talking about than most of the audience members do.

▶ *Know the first two or three sentences of your presentation*. The opening lines are crucial; have them down pat. They must be delivered in a confident and relaxed manner. This is where credibility is established with the audience. You can't afford to fumble over the opening lines or say something that may alienate the audience.

▶ *Use the following approach in your presentation*:
  ✓ First, tell them what you are going to tell them (your outline).
  ✓ Then, tell them (the body of your presentation).
  ✓ Finally, tell them what you told them (your summary).

▶ *Talk to the audience, not at it*. Maintain as much eye contact with the audience as possible, and refer to your notes as little as possible (you'll be glad you practiced plenty of times beforehand).

▶ *Speak clearly and confidently*. Don't speak too quickly or too slowly. Speak in short, understandable sentences—not long, complex, rambling sentences. Pause appropriately after a key point or before moving on to a new item. Use appropriate inflection in your voice to help make a point. Do not present your speech in a monotone.

▶ *Use appropriate animation to help make a point*. Use hand movements, facial expressions, and body language. Don't stand frozen to one spot; move around, if appropriate. In a large auditorium, it's better to have a portable microphone than to be locked to a lectern with a fixed microphone. If you do walk around, whether in a small meeting room or an auditorium, always face the audience when you speak; never speak with your back to the audience. For example, do not face the projector screen and read your visual aid to the audience. Elaborate on the single idea illustrated by each visual aid and give examples, if appropriate.

▶ *Do not stand in front of your visual aids.* Don't stand in a position where you block any of the audience's view of the projector screen, flip chart, or whatever.

▶ *Build interest in your presentation* by developing your "story" with logic and rationale. Gradually increase the tempo of your presentation.

▶ *Keep to the key points in your outline.* Don't digress or wander off the topic or your outline. You will waste time and confuse the audience.

▶ *When making key points, explain to the audience why they are important.*

▶ *Sum up your points on a particular item before moving on to the next item on your outline.*

▶ *Know your closing lines.* The closing is as important as the opening. Tie the closing to the purpose of the presentation. Finish with conviction and confidence.

▶ *Allow time for interaction with the audience, if appropriate.* Ask if there are any questions. You should state at the beginning of your presentation whether there will be time for questions at the end of the presentation or whether the audience can interrupt with questions during the presentation. The latter option can be risky if you have a fixed time slot or an agenda to complete. However, if it's a presentation to a customer conducted in a small meeting room, responding to questions on the fly may be more appropriate than expecting the customer to hold all questions until the end of the presentation. In fact, part of your presentation strategy may be to draw the customer into a discussion to expose his or her opinions.

▶ *When responding to questions, be sincere, candid, and confident.* If you don't know the answer or can't divulge the answer, say so; that's a legitimate answer. Don't be defensive in responding.

Reports

Written reports are just as important as oral reports in communicating information about a project. The required types, content, format, frequency, and distribution of reports that the project organization must prepare may be specified by the customer in the contract.

Some reports may be distributed to a large audience. It's important to know who will be receiving copies of reports. The audience could be very diverse and could include people who are very knowledgeable about the project, as well as individuals who know only what they read in the periodic reports they receive. Recipients of the reports may have different levels of technical sophistication, and some may not understand certain technical language or jargon. It is important to keep in mind that *reports must be written to address what is of interest to the readers, not what is of interest to the person writing the report.*

The following sections discuss two common types of project reports and suggestions for ensuring that reports are useful.

Types of Project Reports

The two most common types of project reports are
- ▶ Progress reports
- ▶ Final report

Progress Reports

It is important to keep in mind that a progress report is not an activity report. *Do not confuse activity with progress and accomplishment.* The customer, in particular, is interested in project accomplishments—what progress has been made toward achieving the project objective-rather than what activities the project team was busy on.

Reports on project progress can be prepared by project team members for the project manager or their functional manager (in a matrix organization), by the project manager for the customer, or by the project manager for the project company's upper management.

Progress reports usually cover a specified period, called the **reporting period.** This period could be a week, a month, a quarter, or whatever best fits the project. Most progress reports cover only what happened during the reporting period rather than cumulative progress since the beginning of the project.

A sample outline for a project progress report is shown in Exhibit 35. Items that might be included in a project progress report include the following:
- ▶ *Accomplishments since prior report*. This section should identify key project milestones that were reached. It could also include a report on achievement (or lack of achievement) of specific goals set for the reporting period.
- ▶ *Current status of project performance*. Data on cost, schedule, and work scope are compared to the baseline plan.
- ▶ *Progress toward resolution of previously identified problems*. If no progress has been made on items brought up in previous progress reports, an explanation should be provided.

▶ *Problems or potential problems since prior report.* Problems can include (1) technical problems such as prototypes that do not work or test results that are not what they were expected to be; (2) schedule problems such as delays encountered because some tasks took longer than expected, materials were delivered late or bad weather caused construction delays; and (3) cost problems such as cost overruns because materials cost more than originally estimated or more person-hours were expended on tasks than had been planned.

▶ *Planned corrective actions.* This section should specify the corrective actions to be taken during the next reporting period to resolve each of the identified problems. It should include a statement explaining whether the project objective will be jeopardized, with respect to scope, quality, cost, or schedule, by any of these corrective actions.

▶ *Milestones expected to be reached during next reporting period.* These goals should be in accordance with the latest agreed-upon project plan.

None of the information in the progress report should be a surprise to the readers. For example, any identified problems should already have been discussed orally prior to the preparation of the written progress report.

Exhibit 35: Project Progress Report Outline for the period September 1 to December 31

1.	Accomplishments since prior report	
2.	Current status of project performance	
	2.1	Cost
	2.2	Schedule
	2.3	Work scope
3.	Progress toward resolution of previously identified problems	
4.	Problems or potential problems since prior report	
5.	Planned corrective actions	
6.	Milestones expected to be reached during next report period	

Final Report

The project final report is usually a summary of the project. It is not an accumulation of the progress reports, nor is it a blow-by-blow story of what happened throughout the project. The final report might include the following:

▶ *Customer's original need*
▶ *Original project objective*
▶ *Customer's original requirements*
▶ *Actual versus anticipated benefits* to the customer as a result of the project

▶ *Degree to which the original project objective was met.* If it was not met, an explanation should be included.

▶ *Brief description of the project*

▶ *Future considerations.* This section could include actions the customer might want to consider in the future to enhance or expand the project results. For example, if the project was constructing an office building, future considerations might be to add a parking deck, a fitness center, or a day care center adjacent to the building. If the project was organizing an arts festival, future considerations might be to change the time of year or to take action to improve the pedestrian traffic flow.

▶ *A list of all deliverables* (equipment, materials, software, documents such as drawings and reports, and so on) provided to the customer

▶ *Test data* from the final—acceptance testing of a system or piece of equipment, on the basis of which the customer accepted the project results

Preparing Useful Reports

Taking into consideration the following guidelines when you are preparing project reports will help ensure their usefulness and value to the recipients:

▶ *Make your reports concise.* Don't try to impress the recipients with volume. The volume of a report does not equate to project progress or accomplishment. If reports are kept brief, there is a better chance that they will be read. Furthermore, report preparation can be a time-consuming activity; the project manager should therefore try to minimize the time needed by the project team to develop input to the project reports.

▶ *Write as you would speak.* Use short, understandable sentences rather than compound, complex, paragraph-length sentences. Long paragraphs will tempt the reader to skip down the page and miss important points. Use simple language that the various recipients will understand. Don't use jargon or acronyms that some readers may not understand. Read the report aloud for content and style. Is it easily readable and understandable, or does it sound stilted and confusing?

▶ Put the most important points first—in the report and in each paragraph. Some readers have a tendency to read the first sentence and then skim over the rest of the paragraph.

▶ *Use graphics where possible*—such as charts, diagrams, tables, or pictures. Remember, a picture is worth a thousand words. Don't make the graphics too busy. Have one concept or point per graphic. It's better to have several clean graphics than a single cluttered one.

▶ *Pay as much attention to the format of the report as to the content.* The report should be open, inviting, and organized in a manner that is understandable to the readers. It should not be cluttered or in a small-sized type font that is difficult to read. It should not contain unclear copies of materials or graphics or forms that have been reduced to an illegible size.

Written reports, like oral communication, leave an impression— positive or negative— with the audience. Care and thought should be given to preparing reports, and report preparation should be looked upon as an opportunity to make a positive impression, rather than as a burdensome, time-consuming activity. It may be worthwhile to ask periodically for feedback from the recipients of the reports regarding the usefulness of the reports in meeting their needs and interests and to solicit any suggestions they might have for enhancing the reports.

Project Documentation and Controlling Changes

In addition to project reports, many other documents may be created by either the contractor's project team or the customer during the project. Some examples are a map of tent locations at a campground for a scout camping trip, assembly instructions for booths for a town festival, drawings for a house addition, and a printout of a computer program for controlling the movements of a robot. Project documents can be text, drawings, forms, lists, manuals, photographs, videotapes, or software. They can be on large paper (for example, an engineering drawing or blueprints) or on a computer disk or CD-ROM (for example, a document or software).

Revisions to project documents can result from changes initiated by the customer or by the project team. Some changes are trivial; others are major, affecting the project work scope, cost, and schedule. An example of a minor change is updating the drawings and assembly instructions for festival booths because a benefactor donated canopies for all the booths. An example of a major change is a change in the location, size, and type of some of the windows, requested by the customer upon seeing the house being built. In this case, it's important that the contractor stop work on those particular windows and inform the customer of any additional costs or schedule delays that might be caused by the requested changes. These changes should be documented in writing for the customer, and the customer should approve the changes before work proceeds and any new materials are ordered.

Throughout a project, various project documents will be revised to incorporate changes. It is important for the project team to know which is the latest version of a document, so that they can perform their work correctly based on the most current information and documentation. For example, the buyer wouldn't want the builder to use outdated drawings if the architect had just made revisions that changed the locations of interior walls.

It's good practice to put on each page of each type of document (1) the date of the latest revision, (2) a sequential revision number, and (3) the initials of the person who made the changes. For example, a notation in the lower right corner of a floor plan for an office arrangement may indicate

Rev. 4, 06/20/2010, JD

This means that the latest version of the floor plan is Revision number 4, which was made on June 20, 2010, by John Doe (JD).

Just as important as keeping up to date with revision numbers and dates on documents is timely distribution of updated documents to appropriate people on the project. When changes are made to documents, the updated documents should immediately be given to any project team members whose work will be affected by the changes. Also, when revised documents are distributed, they should be accompanied by a cover memo explaining the changes that were made to the previous document. This will be helpful to people receiving the document—they won't need to go back and compare the new document to the old one and try to find the changes. If only a few changes are made to a document, distribution of the particular pages that were changed may be all that is required. When changes are extensive, though, it may make sense to distribute the entire revised document rather than all the revised pages.

Early in the project, agreement should be reached between the contractor and the customer, as well as between the project manager and the project team, regarding the way changes will be documented and authorized. If changes are consented to orally rather than in writing and there is no indication given of the impact the changes will have on the work scope, cost, or schedule, there are bound to be problems down the road.

Project team members should be careful about casually agreeing to changes without knowing whether they will necessitate additional person-hours. If the customer does not agree to pay for extra person-hours, the contractor must absorb the costs and risk overrunning costs for a particular task or the project.

Key Project Documentation

Proper documentation – like communication – is a critical support function of project management. And because each project is unique, no specific level of detail is appropriate for all projects. However, there are certain fundamental – or foundational – documents that most project managers will agree are useful.

Several of the documents we'll be reviewing in this chapter have been presented in earlier chapters. What we will do here is provide a framework of understanding about documentation: when certain documents are used, why they are important, and how they relate to one another.

In chapter 1, we discussed what occurs in each of the four major phases of a project: initiation, planning, execution, and closeout. We'll examine common project documents from that same life cycle perspective, considering the documents typically used in each phase.

Initiating Documents

During the first phase of a project, the initiation phase, the project is created, defined in a limited way, officially sanctioned, and launched. This phase begins when a problem or opportunity (i.e., a need) is recognized. An appropriate response to the need is determined and described. (this is actually where the project begins). The major deliverables and the participating work groups re identified. The project team begins to take shape. Issues of feasibility (can we do the project?) and justification (should we do the project?) are addressed and formal approval to proceed is Granted.

Project Requirements Documents

This is perhaps the most fundamental document of you project, as this is where project "life" begins. The Project Requirement Document describes and quantifies the fundamental problem to be solved or opportunity to be exploited (the project need).

▷ *Voice of the customer analysis or market analysis.* Voice of the customer (VOC) refers to the process of capturing customer or user input. The voc approach uses interviewing techniques to better understand what the customer wishes and desires or to solicit input opinions, perceptions, and references. You may or may not choose to use this specific approach. However, the results of any meetings or interviews with customers or user groups should be fully documented and maintained for reference by the project team and other interested parties. In lieu of a voc analysis, a marketing study may be performed; the key difference is that market analysis doesn't focus on interviewing as the sole source of customer input.

Project Definition Document

The project definition document is essentially a response to the project requirements document. The project requirements document describes a problem; the project definition document describes the solution. It, too, is a foundational project document that can be constructed in various ways. However, it should contain certain specific elements.

▶ *Statement of work.* The statement of work is a narrative document that describes the proposed project solution and outlines in limited detail the work to be done. It often includes a listing of major project deliverables, the general approach or methods for doing the work, and how success will be measured. It is the "what" component of the project definition.

▶ *Preliminary project execution plan.* Just as the statement of work describes what is to be accomplished, the preliminary project execution plan describes how it is to be accomplished. This precipitates the creation of a rough order of magnitude (ROM) project plan. This is the first version of the plan and typically includes a schedule, cost estimate, preliminary resource plan, and many of the same components that the final project plan will include. The key difference is that preliminary project plans are assumed to be relatively imprecise. Uncertainty is very high at the beginning of your project, so you should try to avoid using precise estimates

Project Proposal

It's likely that you'll have to prepare some sort of proposal for management approval. You can construct this proposal in different ways. One of the key elements is the business case.

▶ *Business case (economic analysis).* Many companies prepare a business case or business proposition. (Your organization may have another name for this document) Ordinarily a key supporting document within the formal management proposal described above, it describes the impact that the project is expected to have on the organization from a business standpoint. Business cases often rely heavily upon an economic analysis as a way to select between competing alternatives and to determine whether a particular project is justifiable from a cost-benefit standpoint. Although you may not be intimately involved in performing the economic analysis, you're likely to be a participant and to be asked for input. Whoever prepares the business case, you should secure a copy, make sure you understand it, and keep it in your project file.

Project Charter/Project Authorization Document

You'll probably have to seek formal management approval (outside senior management) before you and your teams get into detailed planning. *Project charter is* the term commonly used to describe the documentation created to support the formal authorization to proceed with the project.

Planning Documents

In the next major phase of the project, the planning phase, the project solution is developed in as much detail as possible. It identifies intermediate work products (interim deliverables) and the strategy for producing them. Formulating this strategy begins with defining the required elements of work (task) and the optimum sequence for execution (the schedule).Estimates are made for the time and money needed to perform the work and when the work is to be done. The question of feasibility and justification surfaces again, as formal approval to proceed with the project is ordinarily sought before continuing.

Work Breakdown Structure

The WBS is perhaps the most foundational planning document; just about every other planning document is an extension of the WBS. The WBS lists and organizes into logical subgroups all of the work (activities) required to execute the project

Network Diagram

The network diagram depicts the sequence of the activities. It's the natural starting point of the scheduling process and it's a critical document in schedule development

Project Control Schedule (Gantt Chart)

The project control schedule is a time-scaled bar chart. It uses the logic developed in the network diagram, considers the length of time it take to execute individual activities, factors in resource availability, and places everything into calendar time. It's the document of choice for helping the team focus on what needs to be done and when. A project control schedule is used primarily as an internal control document of the project team and some stakeholders. Progress evaluation, variance calculation, and continuous forecasting are all done using the project control schedule

   ▶ *Responsibility assignment matrix.* The responsibly assignment matrix (RAM) is a two-axis chart that shows how work is assigned. It correlates specific elements of work with specific task performers

   ▶ *Schedule estimating worksheets.* Schedule estimating worksheets are directly related to the basis of estimate concept mentioned several times throughout this book. A basis of estimate describes the assumptions and procedures used in arriving at any and all estimates you receive from estimators. Schedule estimating worksheets should include the assumptions, calculations, and other information used to estimate required labor hours and the activity durations you should request copies of these worksheets, place them in your project files, and refer to them when ever you encounter change.

Project Budget (Cost Estimates)

You should prepare a budget for each project; estimates should be provided for each activity and for the total project. These estimates become the basis for cost tracking and control.

▶ *Cost estimating worksheets.* Just like schedule estimating, worksheets, cost estimating worksheets are also related to the concept of basis of estimate. As the title suggests, cost estimating worksheets would include the assumptions, calculations, and other information used to estimate the expenditure required to execute each activity included in your overall project budget. You should have copies of these worksheets, place them in your project files, and refer to them whenever you encounter change.

"Baseline" project plan

The project plan is more than just a schedule. The baseline project plan appears to lead directly into execution. Although this is true from a document flow perspective, the reality is that many organizations require formal management approval before proceeding to project execution. This formal approval is what creates the sense of a "baseline." Referring to this edition as the baseline plan signifies that this is the plan that everyone will work toward, and that this is the plan from which you will measure project variances.

▶ *Potential problem analysis.* Potential Problem Analysis (PPA) is a risk management technique to identify what may go wrong on your project, so that you can take steps to compensate. Although a PPA can be performed at any time, an excellent time is immediately after creating the project plan. The PPA process normally generates a lot of documentation. You should keep copies of these documents in your project files

Execution and Control Documents

During the third phase, the execution phase, the prescribed work is performed. As project manager, you continuously monitor progress and you make and record appropriate adjustments as variances from the original plan. Throughout this phase, the project team remains focused on meeting the objectives developed at the outset of the project. The following describes the key documents that should be created as part of project execution and control.

Purchasing and Contracting Documents

You'll likely have to procure materials and labor on some or all of your projects. The key documents associated with this process include the following:

- ▶ *Material listing*. Description of materials to be purchased
- ▶ *Purchase order (PO)*. Form used to place order for materials with outside suppliers
- ▶ *Request for proposals/ request for quotes (RFPs/RFQs)*. Documents used to solicit proposals form prospective vendors of products or services
- ▶ *Contract*. Legally binding agreements with external suppliers of goods and services

Progress Evaluation

These reports describe the amount of work being accomplished. These documents typically come from two sources:

- ▶ *Team-generated reports*. This is the information you're collecting in your regular team meetings. You should have documents to serve as a record, such a marked-up schedules or filled-in templates.
- ▶ *Systems-generated reports*. If your organization has the capability to store and retrieve project data, such as labor hours or material costs, you should download this data periodically and keep the documents in you project file.

Project Change Notice

There are many names for this critical document, which is used to document and get approval for any significant deviation from the project baseline. At the conclusion of your project, you ought to be able to reconcile the overall deviation between where you ended up and where you told management you'd end up. That reconciliation is embodied in a stack (hopefully short.) of the project change notices.

Project Status Report

You should provide regular update to organizational management, whether through written reports, one-on-one meeting with the project sponsor, or periodic stand-up presentations. It's important that project managers communicate regularly with stakeholders to inform them of the current status of a project and to manage their expectations for a project. Problems may surface if these key people are not well informed of a project's progress, particularly if shareholders have different expectations. In fact, the source of many project conflicts arise not because of actual problems, but because a customer or a stakeholder was surprised by a project's outcome.

Exhibit 36 presents a project status report template. This template shows one format you can use to effectively communicate a project's status to clients, customers, and other stakeholders. The template contains the following fields:

- *Project name*: The name of the project.
- *Project manager*: The project manager assigned to the project.
- *Time period*: The date range covered by the report.
- *Short project description*: A brief description (two or three lines) of the project to remind the reader the major purpose of the effort. This information can be reused in all subsequent reports.
- *Overall status at a glance*: This section allows the reader to quickly gauge the overall health of the project. The questions are worded in such a way so that all answers should be answered Yes for a project that has no problems. Any questions marked No are red flagged so readers will look for more information about a problem.
- *Explanation of items checked No*: An explanation should accompany any status summary lines that were checked No.
- *Significant accomplishments this period*: A list of major accomplishments from the previous reporting period.
- *Planned accomplishments next period*: A list of major planned accomplishments for the next reporting period.
- *Additional accomplishments or highlights not reflected above*: Discuss any items regarding the project that would be of interest to the reader but were not mentioned previously.
- *Attachments*: Attach any report, log, or relative statistic that would be of interest to the reader. Examples of attachments are included in the template.

Exhibit 36
(Name of project)
Project Status Report
Period ending /12/31/2x10

Project manager:
Business unit/customer:
Project description:

Yes	No	Overall status at a glance
		Will the project be completed on time?
		Will the project be completed within budget?
		Will the project deliverables be completed within acceptable quality levels?
		Are scope change requests being managed successfully?
		Are project issues being addressed successfully?
		Are project risks being successfully mitigated?
		Are all customer concerns being addressed successfully?

Explanation of items above checked No:

Significant accomplishments this period:

Planned accomplishments next period:

Additional comments or highlights not reflected above:

Attachments (the following are examples):

▶ Budget and effort hours summary
▶ Earned value
▶ Issue log
▶ Scope change log
▶ Project workplan
▶ Project metrics/statistics
▶ Additional company reporting requirements

Attachments (the following are examples):

- ▶ Budget and effort hours summary
- ▶ Earned value
- ▶ Issue log
- ▶ Scope change log
- ▶ Project workplan
- ▶ Project metrics/statistics
- ▶ Additional company reporting requirements

Project Plan Updates

The overall project plan should be revised on a regular basis to reflect any changes. As activities are completed and new information about the future becomes available, new forecasts should be prepared.

Close-Out Documents

During the close out phase, the emphasis is on verifying that the project has satisfied or will satisfy the original need. Ideally, the project culminates with a smooth transition from deliverable creation (the project) to deliverable utilization (the post-project life cycle). The project customer accepts and uses deliverables. Throughout this phase, project resources (the member of the project team) are gradually redeployed. Finally, the project shuts down)

The following describes the key documents that should be created as part of project close-out

Punch List Management

Near the end of your project you're likely to recognize that there are a number of tasks to be completed in order to bring your project to a successful conclusion. It may make sense to create a small plan around the *punch list* items that would include these documents.

- ▶ *Punch list task listing.* A simple list of the tasks remaining, which you should review with your customer
- ▶ *Punch list responsibility assignment matrix.* It shows who's responsible for executing the punch list tasks.
- ▶ *Punch list schedule.* A schedule that includes only the items on the punch list, which you should review with your customer, so as to avoid surprises.

Customer Documents

The key documents related to handing off the project (and project deliverables) to the customer include the following:

▶ *Operating and maintenance manuals.* If your deliverables include equipment that the customer or user is to place into service, you should provide information on how to operate and/or maintain the equipment as part of the original project agreement.

▶ *Customer acceptance.* This is a critical document. You should always confirm that the customer is satisfied, is ready and willing to accept the deliverables of the project, and considers the project to be formally concluded

Organizational Documents

There are a few key documents that are of interest to your organization at the end of the project, including the following three:

▶ *Performance evaluation and recognition.* You may be asked to provide evaluative reports on the performance of team members, generally by the resource providers who assigned the people to your project. You can use this opportunity to formally recognize the effort of your team members. However, it's often more impressive to create separate documents that can be placed in term members' permanent records.

▶ *Lessoned learned.* This is a technique to transfer the knowledge gained through your project experiences to the rest of your organization. This can take many forms, but it's often a written report that gets circulated across the entire organization

▶ *Closing report.* Some organizations require a formal report that describes how well the project met its original targets, explains deviations from the plan, and tells whether the benefits promised in the original business case are likely to be realized. For technology-rich projects, the organization often expects technical reports, which describe the project team's experiences in using or creating technology

The Project Management Institute (PMI®) and Certifications

Established in 1969 and headquartered outside Philadelphia, Pennsylvania USA, the Project Management Institute (PMI) (www.pmi.org) is the world's leading not-for-profit project management professional association, with more than half a million members and credential holders in 185 countries. PMI published the project management standard, A Guide to the Project Management Body of Knowledge (PMBOK® Guide). PMI members are individuals practicing and studying project management in many different industry areas, including aerospace, automotive, business management, construction, engineering, financial services, information technology, pharmaceuticals and telecommunications. Members and project management stakeholders can take advantage of the extensive products and services offered through PMI. These products and services are described below and are explained in detail throughout the PMI Web site.

Professional Standards

PMI provides global leadership in the development of standards for the practice of the project management profession throughout the world. PMI's premiere standards document, A Guide to the Project Management Body of Knowledge (PMBOK® Guide), is a globally recognized standard for managing projects in today's marketplace. The PMBOK® Guide is approved as an American National Standard (ANS) by the American National Standards Institute (ANSI). PMI is committed to the continuous improvement and expansion of the PMBOK® Guide, as well as the development of additional standards.

Publications

PMI produces three periodical publications for the benefit of individuals in project management. PM Network® is a monthly professional magazine, Project Management Journal® is a quarterly professional journal and PMI Today® is the monthly newsletter of PMI. PMI is the world's leading publisher of project management books, training tools, and learning products. Over 1,000 titles are currently available from PMI's online bookstore.

PMI® Certifications

Since 1984 PMI has been dedicated to developing and maintaining a rigorous, examination-based, professional certification program to advance the project management profession and to recognize the achievements of individuals in project management. PMI's Project Management Professional (PMP®) certification is the world's most recognized professional credential for individuals associated with project management. In 1999, PMI became the first organization in the world to have its Certification Program attain International Organization for Standardization (ISO) 9001 recognition. PMI now offers specific certification for practitioners with different levels of experience.

- ▶ Project Management Professional (PMP)^{SM}
- ▶ Certified Associate of Project Management (CAPM)*
- ▶ Program Management Professional (PgMP)*
- ▶ PMI Scheduling Professional (PMI-SP)*
- ▶ PMI Risk Management Professional (PMI-RMP) *

Project Management Professional (PMP®)

PMP certification is the project management profession's most globally recognized and respected certification credential. The PMP designation tells current and potential employers that a holder has a solid foundation of project management knowledge that can be readily applied in the workplace.

To be eligible for the PMP certification, you must first meet specific education and experience requirements and agree to adhere to a code of professional conduct. The final step in becoming a PMP is passing a multiple-choice examination designed to objectively assess and measure your project management knowledge. This computer-based examination is administered globally.

In addition, those who have been granted the PMP credential must demonstrate an ongoing professional commitment to the field of project management by satisfying PMI's Continuing Certification Requirements Program.

Mission

Initiate, establish, evaluate, maintain and administer professional credentialing programs to promote and support project management professionals and the project management profession.

Goals

1. Establish, implement and maintain global certification standards, policies and procedures for the PM profession
2. Promote and implement professional credentialing and psychometric methods and procedures for certifications in the PM profession
3. Initiate and foster cooperation and collaboration with other project management organizations to promote and sustain excellence in PM standards and methodology

Certified Associate in Project Management (CAPM™)

As project management grows in scope, importance and recognition, so do the related career and certification options available to you. A logical stepping stone to the PMP, and a boon to your overall professional development, is the CAPM. The CAPM is intended for those practitioners who provide project management services but are relatively new to the profession. Obtaining your CAPM can go a long way toward enhancing your employment and/or project assignment responsibilities – and getting you recognized in the workplace. Like the PMP, CAPM candidates must first meet specific education and experience requirements and then pass an examination.

GLOSSARY

ACTIVITY one that always consumes time and may also consume resources. Examples include paperwork, labor, negotiations, machinery operations, and lead times for purchased parts or equipment.

ACTIVITY-ON-ARC a representation of a project in which arcs represent work tasks and nodes establish precedence relationships.

ACTIVITY-ON-NODE a representation of a project in which nodes represent work tasks and arcs define the precedence relationships.

ACTUAL COST OF WORK PERFORMED (ACWP) total costs incurred (direct and indirect) in accomplishing work during a given time period.

ACTUAL FINISH TIME (AFT) the time at which a particular activity is actually completed.

ARC an arrow in a project network that shows precedence.

ANALYSIS OF VARIANCES analysis and investigation of causes for variances between standard costs and actual costs; also called *variance analysis* or *earned value analysis*. A variance is considered favorable if actual costs are less than standard costs; it is unfavorable if actual costs exceed standard costs. Unfavorable variances are the ones that need further investigation for their causes. Analysis of variances reveals the causes of these deviations. This feedback aids in planning future goals, controlling costs, evaluating performance, and taking corrective action. Management by exception is based on the analysis of variances and attention is given to only the variances that require remedial actions.

AS-BUILT DATA the documentation and information that explains how the project was carried out, valuable for understanding the project management process for future new projects, or when the same project needs to be taken up again in the future.

BACKWARD PASS calculation procedure moving backward through the network that determines the latest start and latest finish times for each activity.

BAR CHART *See GANTT CHART*.

BASELINE PLAN the original plan, or roadmap, laying out the way in which the project scope will be accomplished on time and within budget.

BEST AND FINAL OFFER (BAFO) a final price for a project, submitted by a contractor at the request of a customer who is considering proposals from several contractors for the same project.

BETA DISTRIBUTION a probability distribution that is frequently used to calculate the expected duration and variance for an activity based on the activity's optimistic, most likely, and pessimistic time estimates.

BID/NO-BID DECISION an evaluation by a contractor of whether to go ahead with the preparation of a proposal in response to a customer's request for proposal.

BRAINSTORMING a group decision-making technique operating under the rules that no one's idea should be criticized no matter how outrageous it may appear. The basic purpose of the technique is to generate ideas and original thinking. Now managers can use computer software to encourage brainstorming.

BUDGETED COST OF WORK PERFORMED (BCWP) the sum of the approved cost estimates for activities completed during a given period (usually project-to-date). *See also EARNED VALUE*.

BUDGETED COST OF WORK SCHEDULED (BCWS) the sum of the approved cost estimates for activities scheduled to be performed during a given period.

CAPITAL BUDGET a budget or plan of proposed acquisitions and replacements of long-term assets and their financing. A capital budget is developed using a variety of capital budgeting techniques such as the payback method, the net present value (NPV) method, or the internal rate of return (IRR) method. *See also* CAPITAL BUDGETING.

CAPITAL BUDGETING the process of making long-term planning decisions for capital investments. There are typically two types of investment decisions: (1) Selecting new facilities or expanding existing facilities. Examples include investments in long-term assets such as property, plant, and equipment; and resource commitments in the form of new product development, market research, refunding of long-term debt, introduction of a computer, etc. (2) Replacing existing facilities with new facilities. Examples include replacing a manual bookkeeping system with a computerized system or replacing an inefficient lathe with one that is numerically controlled.

CAPITAL EXPENDITURE BUDGET a budget plan prepared for individual capital expenditure projects. The time span of this budget depends upon the project. Capital expenditures to be budgeted include replacement, acquisition, or construction of plants and major equipment. *See also CAPITAL BUDGETING*.

CASH HOLE the most money that will be invested in the project at any point; also called the *maximum exposure*.

COMMITMENT *See **COMMITTED COST***.

COMMITTED COST the funds that are unavailable to be spent elsewhere because they will be needed at some later time to pay for an item, such as material, that has been ordered; commitment; encumbered cost.

CONTINGENCY an amount a contractor may include in a proposal to cover unexpected costs that may arise during a project; management reserve.

CONTROL to compare progress against plan so that remedial action can be taken when a deviation occurs.

COST PERFORMANCE INDEX (CPI) the ratio of budgeted costs to actual costs. CPI=BCWP/ACWP

COST REIMBURSEMENT CONTRACT a contract in which a customer agrees to pay a contractor for all actual costs incurred during a project, plus some agreed upon profit.

COST VARIANCE (CV) an indicator of cost performance. It is any difference between the estimated cost of an activity and the actual cost of that activity. CV=BCWP-ACWP

CRASH COST the estimated cost of completing an activity in the shortest possible time (the crash time).

CRASH TIME the shortest estimated length of time in which an activity can be completed.

CRASHING process of reducing an activity time by adding resources and hence, usually cost.

CRITICAL ACTIVITY an activity that must be achieved by a certain time, having no latitude (slack or float) whatsoever.

CRITICAL PATH longest sequence of activities in a project management network. It determines the earliest completion of project work.

Critical Path Method (CPM) a technique for identifying the critical path and scheduling project activities. See also ***PERT/COST***.

CUMULATIVE ACTUAL COST (CAC) the amount that has actually been expended to accomplish all the work performed up to a specific point in time.

CUMULATIVE BUDGETED COST (CBC) the amount budgeted to accomplish all the work scheduled to be performed up to a specific point in time.

CUMULATIVE EARNED VALUE (CEV) the value of the work actually performed up to a specific point in time; total budgeted cost multiplied by the percent of the work estimated to be complete.

CUSTOMER REQUIREMENTS specifications for a project and/or attributes of a deliverable specified by a customer in a request for proposal. Requirements may include size, quantity, color, speed, and other physical or operational parameters that a contractor's proposed solution must satisfy.

DELIVERABLES the tangible items or products that the customer expects the contractor to provide during performance of the project.

DISCOUNTED CASH FLOW (DCF) TECHNIQUES methods of selecting and ranking investment proposals such as the net present value (NPV) and internal rate of return (IRR) methods where time value of money is taken into account.

DUE DATE the date, specified in a request for proposal, by which a customer expects potential contractors to submit proposals.

DUMMY ACTIVITY fictitious activity with zero activity time used to represent precedence or used whenever two or more activities have the same starting and ending nodes.

DURATION ESTIMATE the estimated total time an activity will take from start to finish, including associated waiting time.

EARLIEST FINISH TIME (EF) the earliest time that an activity can finish based on early start times.

EARLIEST START TIME (ES) earliest time at which an activity may begin. It is the largest of the earliest finish times for all immediate predecessor activities.

EARNED VALUE (EV)

1. A method for measuring project performance. It compares the amount of work that was planned with what was actually accomplished to determine if cost and schedule performance is as planned.
2. The budgeted cost of work performed for an activity or group of activities.

EARNED VALUE ANALYSIS an approach for monitoring project costs and expenses by specifying, on a periodic basis, how far each activity has progressed (% complete) and deriving the value of work completed from this information.

EFFORT DRIVEN SCHEDULING a project scheduling approach that assumes that time and resources are proportionately related, so that by changing resource levels of activities, we can change the duration of their activity times.

EVENTS beginning and ending points of activities. An event is a specific point in time. Events are commonly denoted graphically by a circle and may carry identity nomenclature (e.g., words, numbers, alphanumeric codes).

EXCEPTION A variation from a customer's specified requirements, stated by a contractor in a proposal.

EXPECTED DURATION the expected duration for an activity, calculated from the activity's optimistic, most likely, and pessimistic time estimates; also called the mean or average duration.

EZPERT a proven software product which is used to automatically generate diagrams, showing Cost, Schedule and Resource information for project management. It prints a Work Breakdown Schedule (WBS) after schedule data have been entered.

FINISH EVENT See *SUCCESSOR EVENT*.

FIXED PRICE CONTRACT a contract in which a customer and a contractor agree on a price that will not change no matter how much the project actually costs the contractor.

FLOAT See *TOTAL SLACK*.

FORECASTED COST AT COMPLETION (FCAC) the projected total cost of all the work required to complete a project.

FREE SLACK (FS) the amount of time that a particular activity can be delayed without delaying the earliest start time of its immediately succeeding activities; the relative difference between the amounts of total slack for activities entering into that same activity. It's always a positive value.

FUNCTIONAL MANAGER the manager that leads a specific work group or team, such as marketing, engineering or software development; also called a *functional supervisor*.

FUNCTIONAL ORGANIZATION STRUCTURE an organizational structure in which groups are made up of individuals who perform the same function, such as engineering or manufacturing, or have the same expertise or skills, such as electronics engineering or testing.

GANTT CHART graphical representation of a schedule used to plan or monitor progress.

INDIRECT COSTS See *OVERHEAD*.

INTERNAL RATE OF RETURN the rate earned on a proposal. It is the rate of interest that equates the initial investment with the present value of future cash inflows.

LADDERING a method of showing the logical precedential relationship of a set of activities that is repeated several times consecutively.

LATEST FINISH TIME (LF) latest time at which an activity must be completed without holding up the complete project.

LATEST START TIME (LS) latest time at which an activity must begin without holding up the complete project.

LIFE-CYCLE COSTING a costing approach that tracks and accumulates all product costs in the value chain from research and development, design of products and processes through production, marketing, distribution, and customer service.

MILESTONE an event that represents a point in a project of special significance. Usually it is the completion of a major phase of the work. Project reviews are often conducted at milestones.

MOST LIKELY TIME ESTIMATE the time in which an activity can most frequently be completed under normal conditions.

MURPHY'S LAW a law stating that 'whatever can go wrong, will go wrong."

NET PRESENT VALUE the difference between the present value of cash inflows generated by the project and the amount of the initial investment.

NETWORK a graphical representation of a project plan showing the relationships of the activities; also called *arrow diagrams.*

NODE an element of a project network that establishes the precedence relationships among the tasks.

NONCRITICAL PATH in a network diagram, any path of activities with a positive value of total slack.

NORMAL COST the estimated cost of completing an activity under normal conditions, according to the plan.

NORMAL PROBABILITY DISTRIBUTION a bell-shaped distribution of values that is symmetrical around its mean value.

NORMAL TIME the estimated length of time required to perform an activity under normal conditions, according to the plan.

OBJECTIVE the expected result or product of a project, usually defined in terms of scope, schedule, and cost.

OPTIMISTIC TIME ESTIMATE the time in which an activity can be completed if everything goes perfectly well and there are no complications.

OVERHEAD a percentage of the direct costs of a particular project, added to a contractor's proposal to cover costs of doing business, such as insurance, depreciation, general management, and human resources; indirect costs.

PARKINSON'S LAW laws advanced by C. Northcote Parkinson in satirical accounts of the administration procedures of business and public organizations. The laws are: (1) work always expands so as to fill the time available for its completion and (2) expenditure rises to meet income.

PAYBACK PERIOD the length of time required to recover the initial amount of a capital investment; also called *time to money* or *breakeven point.*

PERT/COST technique designed to assist in the planning, scheduling, and controlling of project costs; also called the *Critical Path Method (CPM).*

PESSIMISTIC TIME ESTIMATE the time in which an activity can be completed under adverse conditions, such as in the presence of unusual or unforeseen complications.

PLANNING the systematic arrangement of tasks to accomplish an objective; determining what needs to be done, who will do it, how long it will take, and how much it will cost.

PRECEDENCE DIAGRAMMING METHOD (PDM) a type of network planning technique.

PRECEDENTIAL RELATIONSHIP the order in which activities must be finished before other activities can start.

PREDECESSOR EVENT the event at the beginning of an activity (tail of the arrow) in the activity-on-the-arrow form of network diagramming; start event.

PROBLEM a gap between where you are and where you want to be, with obstacles existing that block seamless movement to close the gap.

PROGRAM a large, long-range objective that is broken down into a set of projects.

PROGRAM EVALUATION AND REVIEW TECHNIQUE (PERT) a useful management tool for planning, coordinating, and controlling large complex projects such as formulation of a master budget, construction of buildings, installation of information systems, and information technology (IT) projects.

PROJECT a temporary endeavor undertaken to create a unique product or service. It is the response to a need, the solution to a problem.

PROJECT CONTROL regularly gathering data on actual project performance, comparing actual performance to planned performance, and taking corrective measures if actual performance is behind planned performance.

PROJECT LIFE CYCLE the four phases through which a project moves—identification of a need, problem, or opportunity; development of a proposed solution; implementation of the proposed solution; and termination of the project.

PROJECT MANAGEMENT all activities associated with planning, organizing, scheduling, controlling, and leading a project to ensure that all tasks are completed and that the project delivers its intended results.

PROJECT MANAGER the individual ultimately responsible for the success or failure of a project.

PROJECT NETWORK a graphical characterization of the interrelationships of the work breakdown structure of a project to show the order in which the activities must be performed.

PROJECT ORGANIZATION STRUCTURE an organization structure in which each project has its own project manager and project team and all the resources needed to accomplish an individual project are assigned full-time to that project.

PROJECT SCOPE all the work that must be done to accomplish the project's objective to the customer's satisfaction; scope of the project; work scope.

PROJECT STAKEHOLDER anyone who has a vested interest in their project. These include contributors, customers, managers, financiers, and investors.

PROPOSAL a document, usually prepared by a contractor, that outlines an approach to meeting a need or solving a problem for a potential customer.

PUNCH LIST a relatively small list of tasks that the project team needs to complete in order to close out the project.

REPORTING PERIOD the time interval at which actual project performance will be compared to planned performance.

REQUEST FOR PROPOSAL (RFP) a document, usually prepared by the customer, that defines a need or problem, requirements, and expectations.

REQUIRED COMPLETION TIME the time or date by which a project must be completed.

RESOURCE LEVELING a process that attempts to minimize the fluctuations in requirements for resources across the project without extending the project schedule beyond the required completion time.

RESOURCE LIMITED SCHEDULING a method for minimizing the project duration when the number or amount of available resources is fixed and cannot be exceeded.

RESOURCE LOADING a process for determining the amounts of resources that an existing schedule requires during specific time periods.

RESOURCE SMOOTHING *See RESOURCE LEVELING*.

RESPONSIBILITY MATRIX a table that lists the individuals or organizational units responsible for accomplishing each work item in a work breakdown structure.

RISK ASSESSMENT the combination of risk identification and risk quantification, the primary output of a risk assessment is a list of specific potential problems or threats.

ROOT CAUSE the fundamental cause of a problem in a process. Usually a problem occurs in a process because something went wrong in the immediately preceding step or steps. However, this is the not the root cause. The root cause may have been something that happened much earlier and caused a chain reaction that resulted in the problem being now addressed.

SCHEDULE a timetable for a project plan.

SCHEDULE PERFORMANCE INDEX (SPI) the ratio of work performed to work scheduled. SPI=BCWP/BCWS

SCHEDULE VARIANCE (SV) any difference between the scheduled completion of an activity and the actual completion of that activity.   SV=BCWP-BCWS

SCOPE OF THE PROJECT *See PROJECT SCOPE*.

SLACK length of time an activity can be delayed without affecting the project completion date. *See also TOTAL SLACK*.

SOLUTION-JUMPING the tendency to jump into what to do before analyzing the situation or problem sufficiently.

STANDARD DEVIATION a measure of the dispersion, or spread, of a distribution from its expected value; the square root of the variance.

START EVENT *See PREDECESSOR EVENT*.

STATEMENT OF WORK (SOW) a document outlining the overall vision, goals, objectives, scope, responsibilities, and deliverables of a project.

SUCCESSOR EVENT the event at the end of an activity (head of the arrow) in the activity-on-the-arrow form of network diagramming; finish event.

SYSTEMS DEVELOPMENT LIFE CYCLE (SDLC) a project management planning tool consisting of a set of phases or steps to be completed over the course of development of an information system.

TARGET COSTING a pricing method that involves (1) identifying the price at which a product will be competitive in the marketplace, (2) defining the desired profit to be made on the product, and (3) computing the target cost for the product by subtracting the desired profit from the competitive market price.

TASK (ACTIVITY) specific work that must be accomplished as part of a project.

TASK DEPENDENCY the relationship between two tasks in which the start or finish of the successor task depends on the predecessor task's start or finish.

TEMPLATE a worksheet or computer program that includes the relevant formulas for a particular application but not the data. It is a blank worksheet that we save and fill in the data as needed for a future forecasting and budgeting application.

TIME ESTIMATE *See **DURATION ESTIMATE**.*

TOTAL BUDGETED COST (TBC) the portion of the entire project budget that is allocated to complete all of the activities and work associated with a particular work package.

TOTAL SLACK (TS) Also called *float*. If it's a positive value, it's the amount of time that the activities on a particular path can be delayed without jeopardizing completion of the project by its required completion time. If it's a negative value, it's the amount of time that the activities on a particular path must be accelerated in order to complete the project by its required completion time.

USEFUL LIFE the period of time over the financial analysis of a project will be conducted. It is typically the function of the anticipative economic life of an asset or the expected size of a market window.

VARIANCE
1. A difference of revenues, costs, and profit from planned amounts.
2. A measure of the dispersion, or spread, of a distribution from its expected value.

WEIGHTED FACTOR SCORING MODEL a comparative method for selecting the preferred alternative based upon certain predetermined attributes. Although it does not provide absolute verification of justification, it offers a way to select among alternatives.

WORK BREAKDOWN STRUCTURE (WBS) a hierarchical tree of work elements or items that will be accomplished or produced by the project team during the project.

WORK ITEMS individual pieces of a project in a work breakdown structure.

WORK PACKAGE the lowest-level item of any branch of a work breakdown structure.

WORK SCOPE *See **PROJECT SCOPE**.*

Index